Praise for
Return to Paris

"Rossant explor[es] the wonders of French cuisine [and] shares recipes throughout the book, interspersing them among anecdotes. Those interested in food will enjoy Rossant's careful explanations of meals and markets."

—*Publishers Weekly*

"Rossant's mouth-watering descriptions of her most memorable meals . . . [are] sensuously alive."

—*Library Journal*

"[D]elightful. . . . The highest praise I can give this is to quote the words of distinguished American food critic Homer Simpson: 'Ummm! Fo-o-o-od. Gooood!'"

—*The Washington Times*

"This second part of Rossant's memoirs continues the tradition of interspersing text with recipes for dishes both simple and complex, from *pain perdu* to a whole goose and its artfully stuffed neck."

—*Booklist*

"Rossant writes with such engaging warmth and humanity that the reader is instantly drawn into the rites of passage of a schoolgirl in Paris, whose mixed heritage is difficult but whose love of food ripens into the fruitful loves of a grown woman."

—Betty Fussell, author of
The Story of Corn and *My Kitchen Wars*

"[F]illed with evocative prose and delightful recipes. . . . [Rossant's] love affair with food blossoms into human love in this beautiful and passionate tale of life on the cusp of adulthood."

—Joan Nathan, author of *The Foods of Israel Today*
and *Jewish Cooking in America*

"We must be grateful to Colette Rossant's narcissistic mother. She drove her daughter to the kitchen for companionship. *Return to Paris* is a brilliant coming-of-age food memoir set in the then gastronomic capital of the world. I've never read anything that so beautifully evokes how a palate is cultivated."

—Patricia Volk, author of *Stuffed*

Praise for
Apricots on the Nile

"This is the kind of writing about food that stimulates your senses and connects you to the important traditions of the table. . . . I am enchanted by this memoir."

—Alice Waters

Also by Colette Rossant

Apricots on the Nile: A Memoir with Recipes

Colette Rossant

Return to Paris

A Memoir

WASHINGTON SQUARE PRESS
NEW YORK LONDON TORONTO SYDNEY

Washington Square Press
1230 Avenue of the Americas
New York, NY 10020

ISBN: 978-0-7434-3968-8

First Washington Square Press trade paperback edition April 2004

10 9 8 7 6 5 4 3 2 1

WASHINGTON SQUARE PRESS and colophon are
registered trademarks of Simon & Schuster, Inc.

Manufactured in the United States of America

For information regarding special discounts for bulk purchases,
please contact Simon & Schuster Special Sales at 1-800-456-6798
or business@simonandschuster.com

A postcard from Paris: To Jimmy with love, Colette

Contents

Return to Paris

1

Departure

The windows in my study are wide open; I am looking down at the garden. The cherry tree is in full bloom and from above it looks like a very light white cloud. I remember when we planted it thirty years ago. Juliette, my daughter, wanted a small cherry tree for her birthday. We planted what we believed was a miniature cherry tree. To our surprise it grew nearly sixty feet high and produced great, dark Bing cherries. Juliette loves the tree and thinks that when and if we sell the house, she will cut down the tree and use its wood to make furniture.

The mailman has just delivered a letter, which I hold in my hands. I am not sure I want to open it. I know in my heart of hearts the news will not be good. I am a witch, as I always tell my children; I am sure that this letter bears no good news.

I go back to my desk, letter still unopened. I can hear my grand-

children laughing on the floor above, and as I sit down at my desk, I take out my mother's old photo album and gaze at a photograph of her. She is so beautiful in her long dress. Her train is artfully arranged around her feet. She carries an enormous bouquet of cascading flowers. There are also pictures of my handsome father and of my grandmother, elegant in a large hat and a long dress, holding on to my grandfather and staring boldly out with icy eyes.

I remember my French grandfather's round belly, a pince-nez perched on his nose and a mustache of which he was very proud. I remember walking with him in the park, holding his hand; his picking me up on our walk in the summer to grab hazelnuts from the tree in the back of their summer house. There is a lovely picture of my husband and me when we first met. I look so happy and French; he looks so American!

My grandfather is dead. He died the last month of the war. My mother is also dead. I want to cry.

I open the letter and read the doctor's note. The biopsy is positive. I have breast cancer. . . . Could I call him right away to make an appointment for surgery? I stand there, silent, and then turn back to the photo album to take one more look. I find a picture of me on the deck of the boat taking me from Egypt to Paris. I look forlorn and sad. I close the album and remember.

I am standing on the bridge of a Greek ship, which will take us to Marseilles, looking down at the pier. The noise is deafening, and people are running and passing baggage, crying out in

Arabic: "Be careful . . . turn right . . . No, I mean left . . . . You idiot! Why can't you be more careful!" as they are loading possessions and themselves onto the deck. Families are gathered in a corner saying goodbye to those leaving. Most of the passengers look young. I imagine that, like me, they are going to Europe to study. The war has been over now for nearly two years and the Mediterranean, which had been mined by the Germans, is now declared safe. I am going back to Paris with my mother to attend a lycée and to see my brother, who has spent the war years in France. We are going to live with my maternal grandmother, who has raised my brother. I am excited to go back to France where I was born, although quite sad to leave my Egyptian grandparents and Egypt, where I have spent eight wonderful years.

My mother was French and my father Egyptian. For the first six years of my life we lived in Paris and summered in Biarritz with my maternal grandparents. But in 1937 my father became quite ill with lung cancer. After a successful operation we were summoned to Cairo by my Egyptian grandfather. He believed that my father would recover if the family surrounded him. We arrived in Cairo, greeted by a noisy, affectionate, extended Sephardic Jewish family. We settled down in my grandparents' apartment on the ground floor of their four-story house, surrounded by a large garden with a resplendent mango tree planted, my grandfather liked to say, when I was born. The life of the household revolved around my grandfather, a stern but loving man, and my grandmother, a diminutive woman who

ruled the household and her brood with an iron fist. My voluptuous, attractive mother, happy to be relieved from her duty of
taking care of a sick husband, made herself the toast of Cairo
society. As for me, I spent my time roaming the house, usually
ending up in the kitchen where Ahmet, the cook, prepared
meals that reflected the complex cultural makeup of the family.
I spent a lot of time in the kitchen, tasting Ahmet's food and listening to the kitchen gossip. Warm spices, pungent herbs,
exotic fruits, and the alchemy of hands became part of my daily
life. Within a year, though, my life was shattered for the first
time. My father died. A few months later, my mother decided
that her best life was elsewhere, and left me with my grandparents for the next four years. I was devastated and heartbroken.
Ahmet and his kitchen became my only solace as he enveloped
me with love and food.

In 1942 Cairo had become the center of the North African
war effort. It was a bustling city occupied by the English,
swarming with foreigners and immigrants who escaped the hor-
rors of the war in Europe. My mother, attracted by the glamour
and excitement of Cairo, suddenly reappeared in my life and
yanked me away from the security of my grandparents' home
with the idea of taking care of my education. Since my attachment to her had transformed itself into resentment, our relationship in the beginning was tense and difficult. Desperate to
have a mother like the other children in the family, I tried to
reopen my heart to her. Caught up in the swirl of Cairo's social
life, my mother quickly tired of the mother role she was playing

and stuck me in a convent school for three years, hoping to convert me to Catholicism while she traveled from resort to resort playing cards, dancing, and flirting. To please her and win her love and attention, I did convert, to the chagrin of my Jewish grandparents who felt betrayed by my mother. During those three years I was shuttled between two households, living a difficult double life between an indifferent mother and loving but powerless grandparents. The convent, a squat, five-story house surrounded by gardens just outside Cairo's city limits, had become my haven. The nuns, or *mères* (mothers) as they were called, were warm and tried to make me feel at home. I especially loved Mère Catherine de Rousiers, a young nun full of vitality and good humor who had taken me under her wing. She was the only person I could really talk to about the problems faced by a young teenager—problems that my own mother, who was never there, could not help me solve.

In 1947 my mother, pressured by her own mother in Paris, decided to go back to Paris to be with my older brother, Eddy, whom she had not seen for eight years. She was permitted by my Egyptian grandparents to take me along only after she convinced them that I was in dire need of a proper French education. It was an argument that my grandfather could not ignore; his own children had been educated in Europe. In reality, she was obeying her own mother, who insisted that she finally assume her child-rearing responsibilities. In 1939, my brother had been unhappy in Cairo. He hated the heat, the noise, and especially seeing my father paralyzed and ill. My French grandfather suggested that my brother be sent to France for the summer months, and my mother agreed. The war broke out two months later, but my grandfather, thinking that the war would last just a few months, thought that my brother should stay there. My mother consented, although her decision would create the same nagging resentment in my brother, too. Now that the war was over, my mother had no excuse for not coming back to Paris.

As I stand on the bridge there is a light breeze, and I feel cold and lonely. I look with envy at a young man being hugged and kissed by many relatives down below on the pier. I have no friends here to wave me goodbye, no family below to wish me a safe trip. My grandparents have not come, crushed by the idea of my departure. I shiver at the memory of my grandmother's tearful embrace as she hugged me tightly. I wrap myself in my light wool coat that my grandmother had had made for me, fearing the cold of Paris after being accustomed to the warmth of Cairo. The coat feels heavy on my shoulders from the gold links my mother has sewn into the hem. The government does not allow us to move funds from Cairo to Paris. My grandfather had a long, heavy gold chain made. It is about two meters long, and at his suggestion it is sewn into the hem of my coat. "She is young," he tells my mother, "no one will know. Don't worry. When you reach Paris, here is the name of one of my friends, an Egyptian jeweler. He will sell it for you." There are also gold coins sewn into my shoulder pads. I am a walking golden child. Years later, when I was at the Sorbonne and totally broke, I wore that same coat. I decided one day to remove the shoulder pads, no longer fashionable, and found twelve gold coins hidden in them that my mother had forgotten to take out. I sold six of them immediately and kept six of them. I still have them. One day, I will give them to my grandchildren. As for the chain, my mother sold it when we got to Paris but kept a small piece as a bracelet in memory of our trip. I also have the bracelet. I never wear it as it makes my wrist black because it must be at least twenty-four carats. "You should sell it," my husband tells me once in a while. I seem to be unable to do so, nagged by a superstitious notion that if I do, I will cut all my ties with my childhood. The bracelet stays in my jewelry box. I take it out from time to time and remember.

A loud siren pierces the air and the shouts and cries below intensify. I hear a voice crying, *"Semit, semit."* I look down and see a young boy with a basket on his head filled with *semits*, the Egyptian version of a soft pretzel. I suddenly remember my first bite of the hot *semit* topped with roasted sesame seeds when we first came to Egypt. I run down the plank to buy some while the sailor shouts in Greek to come right up as the boat is about to leave. The soft *semit* tastes wonderful. I don't know then that I will have to wait twenty-five years to eat another one. The loud siren pierces the air again. It is time for the boat to leave, and the people on the pier below look like ants trying to find shelter. I look up to see my mother smiling and talking to the captain on the upper deck. I feel a pinch in the middle of my stomach as I realize that I will probably not see much of her during the trip. She is already flirting and will probably befriend the other officers, who are Greek and Italian. She speaks both languages and will have, I feel sure, a great time becoming the belle of this boat.

As the ship slowly leaves the shore, I look with anger at my mother. I want to go back to Cairo. I am afraid of what lies ahead. What will it be like? I don't even remember my brother. The only thing I remember is that we did not get along. And my French grandmother? What was she like? I have no recollection. I only know stories that I have overheard. My mother and her mother were not close. It seems that my grandmother got along only with her son. I recall someone in the family saying that my mother was afraid of her. She even got engaged to someone she did not like just to get away from her mother. I think it is her father who broke it up, realizing that she really did not love the man. She met my father at Mendès-France's (the future prime minister of France) wedding. Mendès-France's wife was Egyptian but had gone to school with my mother. They were best friends. She asked my mother to be a bridesmaid. My father, friends with the bride's family, was also invited to the wedding. Seeing my mother, so the story goes, he fell madly in love with her at first sight.

The boat glides slowly on the deep blue Mediterranean waters. I keep on eating my *semit*, feeling slightly sick as the harbor slowly disappears. It is getting cold and the bridge is slowly emptying; passengers are going to their cabins. My mother, too, has disappeared. I go down one flight to our cabin. Nausea comes over me like a wave as I sit on the corner of the bed. I run back upstairs, and in the open air on the deck I feel better. My mother reappears and wants me to come down belowdecks to have lunch. I follow her, angry with her for not being by my side when the boat left. My mother looks around the large dining room, smiles at people, and seems quite happy. "Stop brooding, Colette," she whispers harshly. "You don't look pretty when you frown." She chooses a table near the captain's table and smiles at him as she sits down. I cannot stand her! Will she ever behave like a mother? I look around and see other passengers with children. A young mother is bending down to whisper something to her son. He smiles and nods. I feel envious and look back at my mother. "Look around," she says with impatience. "There are several young people your age here. . . . You should make friends. Look at that girl there; she is laughing, do you see? Why can't you be like her?" I want to answer but the nausea returns in cold surges. *I don't have a mother and a father like her,* I want to say, but I feel really ill. "I don't want to be like her and I don't want to be here . . . I feel sick!" I run back to the outer deck, my stomach churning and my skin damp. I hate boats! All along the deck sailors are opening chaises longues. I plop myself on one and allow the breeze to settle my stomach and my anxiety. I promise myself that this is how I am going to spend my days and nights. I don't care about my mother and the other passengers. I just want to feel better.

Later in the afternoon my mother reappears and sits next to me. She has brought me sandwiches and looks at me sheepishly, but I am unaffected. "Try to walk on the deck," she says. "The captain says that it should help you. Shall I bring you a book? Do you need anything else?" She walks away and I do not see her until dinnertime. As she sits again near my chair, she begins to ply me with concerned questions and an offer of help. I look at her in astonishment. Why this attention? I am very pleased and smile for the first time. "I can't go down," I say. "I tried, I really tried, but I can't. Can I have dinner here?" Later the captain comes to talk to me with the ship's doctor. There is no medicine on board that will alleviate my seasickness. They bring me blankets, food on a tray; people stop by to talk to me. I feel better all the time. I like being the center of attention, although I feel somewhat uneasy. Am I like my mother after all? I sleep like a lamb and the next day I try again to go down to our cabin. I wash and dress myself, trying very hard to calm my stomach. I don't last long and very quickly I go back to my chaise. One day down and five days to go.

My days are the same. I walk, eat, and sleep on the deck and spend just a few moments in our cabin to wash and change. I am not sure if by now I am still seasick but I love the attention I am getting, especially from my mother. I am also getting used to the Greek food. I like their salad, especially the cucumber yogurt salad. Their *babaghanou* is not as good as my grand-mother's but it will do. I love the soups and this is mainly what I eat.

The day before landing in Marseilles, my mother comes to sit next to me. She looks embarrassed, clasping and unclasping her hands, which she always does when she wants to say something serious. "There is something I must ask you. I don't know how to explain it but . . . you see . . . my mother does not know that we are Catholics. She will be very upset when she finds out." I put down the sandwich I had been eating, feeling a by now familiar wave of cold dampness over my body. I look at her, not quite understanding where this conversation is leading. My

Cucumber Salad

I loved that salad but did not remember how to make it. Juliette, my daughter, went to Greece and came back with this recipe. Peel and thinly slice 1 long Oriental cucumber. (Oriental cucumber is long and narrow and has very few seeds.) In a bowl beat 2 cups regular plain yogurt. Add 1 garlic clove, minced, ½ teaspoon lemon juice, 1 tablespoon oil, and 1 tablespoon chopped fresh mint. Add salt and pepper to taste. Pour the yogurt over the cucumber and refrigerate until ready to serve. Serves 4 to 6.

Avgolemono Soup

This was my favorite soup on the boat because it reminded me of Ahmet, the cook. He had learned it from my grandfather's chauffeur, who was Greek. In a large saucepan bring 2 quarts strong chicken stock to a boil. Add ¾ cup semi de melone, the tiny pasta that looks like melon seeds. Lower the heat and simmer for 15 minutes or until the pasta is done. Correct the seasoning with salt and pepper. In a bowl beat together 2 eggs with the juice of 1 lemon. Stir the egg mixture into the soup and remove immediately from the heat. Allow the soup to stand covered for 5 minutes. Serve immediately. Serves 4.

French grandmother would be upset? But why? Isn't she Catholic?

"You have to promise not to tell her."

"Who?"

"Your grandmother."

"But why? I promised Mère Catherine that I would go to Mass every Sunday. I don't understand! Why is it wrong to tell her?"

My mother sits quietly for a while as I weep. I see myself going to hell, being punished for my sins. I remember my First

Communion, the promises I made, the warmth of the convent, and especially Mother Catherine, who took such good care of me, I long to be back in Cairo. There, there were no lies. My Jewish grandparents knew about the convent and my conversion. We never talked about it, but there was a tacit understanding about freedom of choice, which my mother then refused to acknowledge. I look at my mother; her skin is dry and her eyes are opaque with annoyance and fear. I suddenly realize that my mother has converted to Catholicism and that she, too, came from a Jewish family. I had heard my aunts, grandmother, and grandfather talk about the problems facing the Jews in Europe. Whenever I would approach or try to listen they would suddenly stop talking. My cousins and I thought that whatever was happening in France was dreadful, but we didn't really comprehend the gravity of the situation and wondered constantly. Cairo had a great number of European Jews who had escaped the war, and stories about their hardships reached my family. At this particular moment I felt confused and for the first time I found myself wondering what I *was*—Catholic or Jewish? Could I erase the fact that I had been born Jewish? I desperately wanted to be Catholic. Would my grandmother force me to abandon what I had been taught? Why was my mother scared of her?

"Just promise me you will not say anything. The war was hard on her and Eddy and it would make everything worse if we tell."

I look at her again and realize that once more she has

betrayed me. I also know now, feeling her fear growing into panic, that I can ask for anything in exchange for my promise. "I will not tell but you must promise that you will stay in Paris and not go back to Cairo without me."

"I promise," my mother says with relief.

For the last two days of the trip, my mother takes care of me, reading books aloud and talking of the things we would do together. I am so happy that I start to forget about her mother and my fears slowly disappear. On the first of June, 1947, our ship anchors in Marseilles. I stand on the bridge looking down onto the pier. The atmosphere is not the same as in Alexandria. Less shouting and pushing, and the pier looks cleaner. People are standing there waiting for the passengers to get off. My mother is looking for someone in the crowd. "There she is," my mother says. "The tall lady with the hat. Wave, Colette, so she can see you." I look down at the tall woman in an elegant black dress with a large hat waving back. She does not look so terrifying, and I feel better.

The boat is slowly unloading. Suddenly my mother screams, *"Faites attention, regardez où vous allez!"* (Be careful, look where you are going.) Along the plank an enormous burlap sack is being unloaded. Suddenly, the bag rolls and falls with a large thud onto the pier, bursting open. *"O, mon Dieu!"* My mother sighs with disgust. "There goes the rice!" And the kilos of rice that my mother, at her mother's request, had packed to bring to France where food was still scarce and rationed, has spilled out everywhere. I see people running with paper bags, picking up as much rice as they can. To my mother's chagrin, we end up with only a small bag of rice.

At the bottom of the plank stands Grandmaman Rose, looking at me and smiling. "You're not very tall," she says, "but you have very nice hair. Come . . . let's get to the station and home." She takes me by the hand and, followed by my mother, we walk to the exit and to what I think will be a new and marvelous life.

The train ride to Paris was interminable. We all sat in a second-class compartment on hard seats, wilting in the close, hot air. My mother didn't dare complain as yet. The two women, voices shrill with tension, talked together and ignored me. My brother, Eddy, was the first topic of conversation. Grandmaman Rose boasted of his success in school, how he had passed his baccalaureate at the age of sixteen, one of the youngest students in France to do so. "He is planning to be a chemical engineer," she preened. "He loves music, you know." She paused so that we might absorb his grandeur, then added gravely, "But why *would* you know?" I saw my mother's face become chalky and her hands tighten their clasp on each other, so I did something that soon became a habit in her presence. I started to chat about anything that came to mind. I talked about the crossing, about the dark Greek sailors, about some of the more colorful passengers. My grandmother laughed, the atmosphere of our compartment relaxed, and my mother smiled at me as if to say thank you. I felt like an actress who had just won her audience.

The journey was slow due to mines on the tracks. During the war, my grandmother told us, the *cheminots* (railroad workers) sabotaged the Germans by derailing trains en route to Germany. "Not only the trains carrying Jews to concentration camps, mind you, but also French workers who were obliged to work in German factories," she explained. My mother's look turned sheepish, as it often did in the next few months, at the mention of what the Jews—and by implication what her mother and son—had suffered during the war. My dread at the lie I was to live returned as I looked at my grandmother's slight smile of satisfaction at having just humiliated her daughter. To dispel this embarrassing moment, I announced loudly that I was famished and could we order lunch.

My first meal in France, in a hushed and formerly elegant dining car, was a revelation. The menu was absurdly simple; there was a choice of an *omelette aux fines herbes* or a *sandwich jambon beurre*. I chose the *omelette* and was delighted by the flavors of chives, tarragon, and chervil mingling in the creamy lightness of the eggs, all so new to me. If the food in France was so good even in a train, I thought I might have a happy life here after all. Raspberries laced with streams of crème fraîche sold me on the value of my new adventure. To this day, I have an intense and nostalgic fondness for both dishes. In fact, if my grandson Matthew ever shows an unwillingness to eat at lunchtime, I bring him back to the table with a promise of an *omelette aux fines herbes*.

Omelette aux Fines Herbes

In a bowl beat 6 large eggs until well mixed. In a food processor finely chop 1 tablespoon each of fresh tarragon, fresh chervil, and fresh Italian parsley. Set aside. In a large nonstick skillet melt 2 tablespoons butter. When the butter is bubbling add the eggs. Cook for 2 minutes and lower the heat to medium. With a fork bring the edges of the omelet toward the center. When the omelet is half cooked, sprinkle the top with the herbs, and salt and pepper to taste. Cook for another 2 minutes; then with a spatula fold the omelet in two. Cook for another 2 minutes and slide it gently onto a serving platter. Garnish with 2 tarragon sprigs. Serves 4.

Two hours later I awaken in the recovery room. I am freezing, and nurses fuss over me. I hear them talking as if through a cloud of cotton wool. It seems that my temperature is too low and that they need to bring it up. I am wrapped in blankets, hot water bottles tucked around my body. I want to tell them that I am all right, that I want to see my family and get out of that room. I think I am saying something to the nurses but no sound comes from my lips. I am not as cold and I fall back to sleep. Two hours later, as I am wheeled out of the recov-

ery room, I see and feel my husband kissing me. I feel wonderful. I am alive and he is here, as I knew he would be. I squeeze his hand and smile again because I see my son and my three daughters. This is what I have lived for, fought for. We are the beginning. The room is full of flowers; my children take turns holding my hands, kissing me. I am tired and relieved. The doctor comes into my room and says that the prognosis for full recovery is even better than expected. The lymph nodes are free of cancer. I look around me and think that in three days I will go home and the future does not seem bleak, as I know deep in my heart that I will beat this curse.

2

Paris and My French Family

We *arrived in Paris* in the late afternoon, and from the taxi window, the city seemed dark and forbidding. My grandparents had lived all their lives in the 17th arrondissement, and as we approached their house I could see the Arc de Triomphe garishly illuminated against the twilight. My grandmother explained that in 1945 she had watched a column of American soldiers march down the Avenue de la Grande Armée, her own street! "The most beautiful sight ever," my grandmother mused. "General Eisenhower was at the head of the army, and a military plane actually swooped down and through the Arc de Triomphe to the Champs Elysées." The wide avenue, bordered by handsome chestnut trees, did not impress me. I found the identical façades of the houses shabby and dull. The houses in Cairo, in

Garden City where we lived, had lovely gardens and flowers everywhere. My grandparents had moved several blocks farther away from the arch, and I tried hard to remember their old apartment where I had learned to roller-skate down the long corridor that led to the kitchen where Georgette, cook and confidante, reigned. *She must be old now,* I thought.

The taxi stopped in front of a large green door with brass knobs. My grandmother rang the bell, and the door popped open with a clicking noise onto a large passageway leading to an inner courtyard. The taxi driver dropped our luggage in the hallway and left. I stood in the middle of the hallway and looked around. On my left was the concierge's *loge* or apartment and on the right, glass doors leading to a majestic stairway and an elevator. "Don't stand there like a statue," my grandmother grumbled. "Pick up a suitcase and follow me." The elevator was narrow with a cast-iron outer gate and two glass doors etched with an intricate floral pattern. (A year later I swung myself on the door and the elevator went down, crushing my back. I screamed and the concierge came to rescue me. I was badly bruised and had a broken rib but nothing more. Now, whenever I am in a small elevator with my grandchildren, my eyes are glued to the door with panic.) The apartment was on the third floor. It had two entrances, one on the left and one on the right of the staircase. My brother opened the door before we had a chance to knock and I stood at the threshold, staring and immobile. Eight years is a very long time in the life of a fifteen-year-old. From a cherubic baby brother, he had grown into a tall, thin, mournful adolescent, dressed in ugly brown trousers and a light cotton sweater. He looked to my young eyes ungainly and badly dressed. Of course, I too had changed, and Eddy stared equally hard at me, his eyes moving very fast. Years later I learned that Eddy had an eye problem that my daughter Juliette would inherit. As my grandmother gently asked Eddy to help his mother with the luggage, a tall, thin woman, wearing a flowered dress and a large white apron encircling her narrow body, embraced me, squeezing me hard around the chest. "You look lovely . . . so lovely. I missed you so much . . . look at me! I would have recognized you anywhere . . . same curls . . . same lovely eyes . . ." My grandmother interrupted this litany to ask Georgette to help my brother and mother, who were downstairs with all the heavy bags. Reluctantly Georgette let go of me and ran downstairs while my grandmother pushed me inside the flat. I was tired and overwhelmed by everything and everybody. I let my grandmother lead me to a room. "This is your room for now . . . then we will see." I sat on the bed, bewildered, lonely, wondering how my mother greeted my brother. Did they talk while waiting for Georgette to come and help? Did they embrace? Was he shy? I looked around. The room was small and spare; a massive armoire with carved doors overpowered and darkened the space. The walls were covered with yellow-and-blue–striped wallpaper decorated with small flowers. Above the bed was a large painting of the Place du Tertre in a heavy, carved gilded frame. The desk stood opposite the bed, and from the ceiling hung a bronze chandelier with candle-shaped bulbs that gave off a weak light. I walked to the window overlooking the gray, silent courtyard. I walked back to the bed and sat down, heavyhearted. I missed my own bedroom in Cairo, with its picture window overlooking the mango tree that my grandfather had planted when I was born. There everything was cheerful, light, filled with rich color; here everything seemed heavy, dark, and somber.

I left the room to explore the apartment, which was typical of those belonging to upper-middle-class Parisian families. Overlooking the avenue was a large bedroom, a living room, and a dining room. The back of the house had two smaller rooms and a bathroom. One was the room given to me; the other was my brother's bedroom, which had once been my grandfather's study. I envied Eddy. It was a wood-paneled room with a glass-enclosed library reaching to the ceiling and containing all of my grandfather's books, lots of classic novels, some of my brother's schoolbooks, and a twenty-volume encyclopedia entitled *Je Sais Tout.* (I spent many teatime hours browsing through them, admiring the intricate etchings. My favorite one was of the famous chef Carême, the eighteenth-century French chef, standing next to a *pièce monté* prepared for some king. (I always thought that one day I would try to reproduce that particular masterpiece—three layers of three different cakes, each with intricate designs, the top looking more like a Greek temple than a pastry. I never got past baking a simple tart.) In one corner was a heavy mahogany desk and next to it an enormous dark red armchair, which soon became my haven, and in which I curled up and got lost in novels like *Claudine à l'Ecole* by my namesake, Colette, *Cousine Bette,* and *Le Rouge et Le Noir.* (I got blasted by my grandmother for reading and loving Colette's novels; she would say in a very moral tone, *"Immoral . . . Pas pour une jeune fille de bonne famille.")* Against the wall was a narrow bed with leather cushions and a fur blanket. Dark walls and a dim chandelier like mine gave the room a cavelike atmosphere.

Between my room and my brother's was the bathroom. In contrast to every other room in the house, it was spacious, airy, and whitewashed, with two sinks, a deep tub, and an awkwardly positioned hot-water heater. The toilet (water closet) was built into the long corridor leading to the kitchen. My grandmother's bedroom had a private entrance and was more elegant and comfortable than any other room. I coveted the Tiffany lamps that adorned her side tables and the tortoiseshell comb atop her dressing table. But the kitchen, Georgette's queendom, was by far my favorite.

I was drawn to it right away, just as I had sought solace in the kitchen of my Cairo childhood. I missed the aroma of the *ful medamas* (braised brown fava beans) warming on our cook Ahmet's stove, and the licks of chocolate mousse that he'd give me off the spoon. I had felt secure and protected in that Arab kitchen, with its spicy smell and Ahmet's attentions. As I entered this new kitchen, I first noticed Georgette, who was standing over a large skillet stirring what smelled like garlic, parsley, and rich butter. I remembered her vaguely as rather plump, but she had grown older and was now very slender under her white butcher's apron, with wavy black hair and huge brown eyes. I approached her shyly, not knowing how to begin a conversation. She smiled at me. "Come, Colette, come near. Let me look at you again." Her wide red lips seemed to take over the bottom part of her face as she grinned. She did not look like a cook. She was beautiful.

The kitchen was a large, brightly lit room with a four-burner stove and a white enameled table covered with the ubiquitous floral waxed tablecloth. (I hated that cloth; it seemed to be perpetually wet and slightly sticky to the touch. I refused to eat on it and would lift it up and eat directly on the enamel table, to my grandmother's chagrin.) An enormous refrigerator dominated the room. My grandmother was very proud of this refrigerator, which she bought in America before the war. Georgette told me that she was the first among her friends to have a refrigerator. Georgette, however, preferred her *garde-manger,* a little cabinet built into the wall beneath the window and open to the outside, with a screen to protect the contents from insects and rain. Georgette hid her treasures there: a pâté made by her sister-in-law, creamy butter from the country, vegetables, yesterday's consommé. "So much better than her refrigerator," Georgette would whisper to me as my grandmother admonished her for not storing everything in her proud possession. Georgette's gleaming copper pots and pans hung from the ceiling, and she polished them religiously. I inherited those pots, and although I don't use them, I polish them myself so that they shine on my kitchen wall, reminding me of Georgette's warm pride and warm heart.

I often caught Georgette talking to the other maids in the building, her head hanging out of the large kitchen window, gossiping about the concierge or the tenant on the fourth floor, a single man with lots of friends. Bets were made when they caught him with a new woman. Was she or wasn't she the one who would catch him? By the time I left home, the man was still unmarried!

The design of our building was the same as for all the buildings on the avenue. In the nineteenth century, Baron Haussemann, Napoléon III's city planner, enlarged the avenue, and for the first time developers built apartment houses whose plans were virtually identical. Facing the avenue were the large, expensive apartments. Behind them was a courtyard, and at the back of it, another building with no elevators and smaller apartments. These were meant for the working class and artisans. In a few days I learned who lived on what floor, how much money they were making, and, more often than not, I learned of their personal problems that were endlessly shared by the other tenants, the concierge and, naturally, Georgette.

"Are you hungry? Can you wait till dinner or would you like something now?" I was famished but what would I ask Georgette for? In Cairo, Ahmet would have heated up a *sanbusak,* a little pastry baked with cheese, or slathered a pita bread with *babaghanou.* I looked at her again silently, trying to remember what she was like when I was six years old and loved her so much. I remembered going to the market with her. She would urge me to smell the fresh herbs by crushing them between her fingers, saying, "Sniff, Colette; this is fresh rosemary for tonight's chicken." And I would put my nose in her fingers and inhale the

Chicken Fricassee

Have the butcher cut 2 small chickens about 2 pounds each into 2-inch pieces. You can also use just chicken legs and thighs. In a casserole melt 2 tablespoons butter and 1 tablespoon olive oil. When the butter is hot add 3 garlic cloves and sauté for 3 minutes. Dust the chicken pieces with flour and add to the casserole. Sauté the chicken until all the pieces are golden brown. Then add 10 small onions and sauté for 5 minutes. Add 1 rosemary sprig and 3 parsley sprigs, tied with a string, and salt and pepper to taste. Add 12 small potatoes and 2½ cups chicken bouillon. Bring to a boil, lower the heat to simmer, cover, and cook for 45 minutes. Remove the rosemary and parsley. Transfer the chicken and the potatoes to a platter. In a bowl beat 2 eggs and slowly add some of the chicken juice, mixing well. Add the eggs to the casserole juices. Heat for 2 minutes but do not boil. Correct the seasoning with salt and pepper. Pour the sauce over the chicken, garnish with chopped parsley, and serve. Serves 6.

lovely fresh aroma of the rosemary. This is what I smelled now. "You have rosemary in that dish; what are you cooking?" "A chicken fricassee with rosemary . . . try the sauce," she said, handing me a wooden spoon filled with a light aromatic *jus*. So delicious. While the chicken was simmering, she sat down next to me with a bowl full of tiny onions and started to peel them. "You add the onions after the chicken is golden brown," she explained. "You still like to cook? You want to help me, peel the potatoes. I will cook them with the chicken." I sat down in front of a bowl of small potatoes, washed and ready to peel. I had never peeled anything before, so Georgette picked up a small paring knife and showed me what to do. As she handed me the knife, she smiled. I felt useful and appreciated and went to work. From time to time Georgette turned around to admonish me. "Not so much skin! And remove the little black spots with the point of your knife!"

I worked in silence, looking at Georgette from time to time. She sautéed the small pieces of chicken in the aromatic oil, then added the onions. Suddenly I heard a loud swish. She was pouring some bouillon into the skillet. I wanted to tell her about Ahmet and the kitchen in Cairo but I felt I had first to reestablish my relationship with her. Suddenly my grandmother appeared in the kitchen. "There you are," she said. "I knew I'd find you here. Come with me and let's unpack your things. You'll help her later." She had never liked to see me in the kitchen when I was little, complaining that I smelled like a kitchen helper. Today, it seemed I could be there without being scolded.

I eagerly followed her to my room. But my mother reappeared and said that she would help me unpack my things. I was sorry to see my grandmother leave; I wanted to be with her. More than anything I wanted her to talk to me. When she left the room we started to unpack. At the bottom of my suitcase was the missal that Mère Catherine of the Convent of the Sacred Heart had given me when I left Cairo. "I didn't want her to see it," my mother said with annoyance. "Where shall we hide it?" She looked tired and nervous, and I felt sorry for her. But why did we have to lie? Would my grandmother really be so angry? She seemed quite nice if a bit stern. Was my mother afraid of my brother? I wondered where he was. I had barely seen him. Was he pleased to see his mother after so many years? Or did he resent her for having left him behind? "Are you dreaming?" My mother's harsh voice interrupted the questions swimming in my head. "Help me, I say. Where shall we hide it?" I looked around the room; there were no shelves, no bookcase, only the armoire where my mother was hanging my clothes. If we hid it in the armoire, my grandmother would find it. Where then? Angry with my mother, I said in a rough tone, "Under the mattress. In the middle of it; she won't see it." My mother looked embarrassed but quickly hid the missal under the mattress. I heard my grandmother's voice calling us to supper. My mother took my hand and squeezed it as if she wanted to let me know she was sorry, and we left the room. She put her arm around my shoulders, something she had never done before. I walked slowly with her toward the dining room, afraid that she would remove her arm. I could feel the warmth of her body near mine. As we approached the dining room, I felt her body stiffen. She dropped her arm and walked quickly in, leaving me behind. I followed her, still angry and a bit afraid. *Why,* I wondered, *is she so scared?*

Above the long table in the dining room hung a magnificent crystal chandelier with a multitude of small, candle-shaped lights. Each arm of the chandelier had long pieces of crystal dangling from it, and the breeze coming in through the French windows made them dance with shards of delicate color infusing the crystal. I stared at it with delight as I sat by my grandmother's side for the evening meal. My brother was on her other side, and I could not see him well. Although my mother asked him countless questions, he spoke very little, answering a yes or a maybe or just a nod of the head. The dinner was delicious. We started with a green soup served with small croutons infused with garlic. *"Un bouillon d'herbes"* (an herb soup), my grandmother said. "The markets are not yet full, and butter, eggs, and cream are rationed. Also, oil and cigarettes." Turning to my mother she asked, "You don't smoke, do you?" As my mother shook her head my grandmother added, "Good, so there is not a problem if we exchange them for something else." I liked the soup and said so in a loud voice. I wanted to get my grandmother's attention and I succeeded. My grandmother explained that the soup had no butter but was made with a strong chicken stock. Only children, she explained, got butter, eggs, and milk every week; grown-ups only once a month. "We have to register

Colette tomorrow so we can get some stamps for her rations. She is a J-3 and that will help the family." A J-3, I learned later, was a child between the ages of ten and eighteen and was entitled to special food stamps. I felt rather important just then and settled happily into the main course, the chicken fricassee with the small potatoes I had peeled. Each piece was lightly napped with a creamy sauce. The dish was succulent. My pleasure was short-lived as my grandmother pushed in front of me a purée of something green. I took one bite and grimaced. I hated spinach and the dish was no better than the one we were obliged to eat at the convent. "I don't want it," I said, pushing the dish away. "I hate spinach." My grandmother frowned and said something that I would hear time and time again. "Eat it! Here, we went through the war and often had nothing to eat. You must eat what is on your plate. You are spoiled." I sat staring sullenly at my grandmother, then at my mother, who said nothing. I did not want to insist and ate the spinach, closing my eyes in disgust.

We had brought with us a crate of oranges from Cairo and the large sweet lemons that I liked so much. As Georgette placed a bowl of oranges in the middle of the table, I reached to pick one for myself. Suddenly my grandmother hit my hand. "Don't do that!" What had I done that was so wrong? "There are very few oranges in Paris. Here you don't eat one by yourself. You share!" I remembered, almost shamefully now, eating oranges in Cairo. My grandfather would roll the orange on the table, pushing it down with the palm of his hand until it felt soft. He'd make a hole at the top and hand it to me. I would bring the orange to my mouth and squeeze. The juice exploded in my mouth, and the seeds stayed in the orange. I loved the cool sweet orange juice. We ate two or three at a sitting. No more! My grandmother peeled the orange and handed me a few segments, then passed some to my mother and brother. *Well,* I thought, *I will get used to that too.*

Later that evening I went to the bathroom to run my bath. In Cairo we had showers, but this bathroom had none. I lit the hot water heater and turned the faucet. The water was filling the bath slowly so I went into my brother's room. He was sitting at his desk, and as I entered he lifted up his head and said grimly, "Knock at the door next time." "What are you doing?" I asked, as I gazed at his pale adolescent face. He looked up at me. His eyes seemed to move quite fast, from one corner to the next. I wanted to ask why but I didn't dare. His eyes were clouded with bitterness. "What do you want?" he asked. "Nothing, just to talk." "I can't talk now; I have a test tomorrow, so leave the room. I have to work." I left the room, intending to look for my mother or Georgette, when I heard my grandmother's voice calling my name from the bathroom. *Oh God,* I thought. *I left the water running. Maybe it has overflowed. What a disaster.* As I entered the bathroom, my grandmother was standing near the bathtub, which was only half full. I let out a sigh of relief. "Never, you hear, never fill the bathtub! Gas is expensive! Only fill it just to there," she said as she pointed to the bottom of the bathtub. *How can I wash myself in so little water,* I thought, but said nothing to her as she left the bathroom. What a day! Everything I was doing was wrong. I hated Paris and I wanted to go back to Egypt!

In the next few days I learned that I was not supposed to take a bath every day. Twice a week was enough. "It is bad for your skin," my grandmother said. "Use the bidet to wash yourself." I thought everyone in my family smelled to high heaven. In the five years I stayed with her I could never get used to the idea of not bathing every day.

The next morning, I woke up thinking I was in Cairo and quickly realized that I was in Paris. I looked out of the window at the courtyard and saw the concierge talking loudly to a woman on the third floor of the next building. They were arguing about the lady's cat, which had torn a garbage bag and made a mess in the courtyard. "It's your damn cat," cried the concierge. "No, I tell you. It's not him. Poucet is nice . . . he was here with me the whole evening." I ran to the kitchen to ask Georgette what was really happening down there. Eddy was sitting at the table having breakfast, a woman's silk stocking thrust down around his head. I burst out laughing. "What's that for?" I asked. "You look like a clown." My brother got up, said, "You stupid girl!" and rushed out of the room. Georgette told me to sit down. She put a bowl filled with steaming café au lait in front of me and next to it, a long piece of baguette spread with butter and jam. "Eat and I will tell you why you should not laugh at Eddy." The bread was fresh, crunchy, and tasty, the raspberry jam rich, and the coffee smoothed with chicory. "Eddy had a hard time here during the war . . . and you know he missed you and your mother. Do you know that his hair is so curly that it stands up after he washes it? He has to put this net on his head to flatten it; if not they will make fun of him." I understood, and thought about my cousins in Cairo, who all had tight curls. I missed them desperately, but I promised not to laugh at Eddy anymore.

The cries of the concierge below intensified. We both ran to the window. "It is the dressmaker on the third floor," explained Georgette. "Every morning the concierge screams at her about her cat. *Pauvre* Mlle Poucet, it is not her fault. I don't think it is her cat. I think it is someone's in the building." As the fight continued, I left the kitchen and went to Eddy's room. I knocked on the door as I had been told. I poked my head through, said "I'm sorry," and waited. Eddy looked at me, smiled, and said, "When I come back from school, I'll take you for a walk." Peace was in the air, and happily I went looking for my grandmother.

The next few days were very busy. The first morning I followed my grandmother to the town hall so I could register and get my J-3 stamps. We went food shopping down the street behind the house, an excursion repeated every morning. Lunch was the main meal of the day, and the aroma of Georgette's cooking would drift through the house. My brother came back for lunch but my mother was often not there. "Where is Line?" my grandmother would inquire of Georgette. My mother was out visiting her old friends, having lunch with them or shopping. She quickly took on her old ways, absenting herself from the household and her children's lives. Food offered me solace. Meals were simple and perfectly executed, each on a particular day. Sunday lunch was a roast leg of lamb stuffed with garlic, cooked medium-rare with a crust of coarse salt mixed with tarragon, a potato purée, and *haricots verts*. Dessert was bought at

Roast Leg of Lamb

With the point of a knife remove the thin white membrane of a 6-pound leg of lamb. Peel 3 garlic cloves and insert slivers of garlic all over the lamb. Melt 3 tablespoons of butter. In a bowl mix together 1½ cups coarse salt with 3 tablespoons chopped tarragon and add 1 teaspoon freshly ground pepper and the butter. Mix well and spread the mixture on the leg of lamb. Place the leg in a roasting pan. Add 1½ cups of water mixed with 1 tablespoon soy sauce. Bake in a preheated 325-degree oven about 15 minutes a pound for medium-rare. Remove from the oven and allow the lamb to rest before carving it. Brush away the salt, carve the lamb, and place on a serving platter. Garnish with chopped tarragon. Degrease the pan juice. Add ½ cup hot water, bring to a boil, and correct the seasoning with salt and pepper if needed. Pour ¼ cup juice over the lamb and serve the remainder in a sauceboat. Serves 6 to 8.

Lentil Salad

To make this salad it is better to use French or Italian small lentils, available in most health food or gourmet stores. Wash 2 cups French or Italian lentils and place them in a saucepan with 4 cups chicken bouillon. Bring to a boil, lower the heat, and cook until the lentils are tender but not overcooked, about 30 minutes. Drain and place in a salad bowl. In a small bowl mix together 1 garlic clove, minced, 1 tablespoon lemon juice, 2 tablespoons olive oil, and salt and pepper to taste. Mix well and pour over the lentils. Toss and set aside until ready to serve. The lentils should be room temperature. Serves 6.

the pâtisserie down the block. Monday was my favorite lunch—cold thin slices of lamb served with a salad of lentils, followed by cheese and fresh fruit. Spring brought *fraises des bois,* wild strawberries no bigger than a nipple, bathed in crème fraîche. Tuesday was chicken day, and every week Georgette made a different chicken dish. The two that I remember still are Georgette's chicken fricassee and a tender poached chicken. Wednesday was the only day that pained me. It was horse day. We were served chopped horsemeat—bloody, sickly sweet, and rather mushy. I battled long and hard for the right to enjoy one of Georgette's *omelettes* as a substitute. Thursday was stew day.

Steamed Leeks

Cut off about 2 inches from the green part of 12 leeks. Trim the tops and wash the leeks under cold running water. Drain. Place the leeks in a large skillet with 1 cup water and ½ teaspoon salt. Bring to a boil, lower the heat, and simmer for 20 minutes, or until the leeks feel tender when pierced with a fork. Serves 6.

The only one I liked was the lamb stew made with lots of small vegetables. I disliked the *queue de boeuf* (oxtail stew), but Georgette served it with steamed leeks, which I adored. Friday was fish day: baked monkfish once in a while, a fish stew, or broiled fresh herrings. On Saturdays, if we were invited to lunch somewhere, Georgette made a *potée,* a mixture of boiled meats and vegetables served with *ailoli,* a very garlicky mayonnaise, so that on Monday we could have cold meats with mustard. Dinner was most often a simple soup, followed by a few slices of French ham with a green salad, cheese, and fruit.

As soon as I grew more confident about my surroundings, my grandmother started to send me shopping in the neighborhood. Avenue de la Grande Armée was one of the large boulevards that started at the Arc de Triomphe. It was lined with tall chestnut trees, and there were three métro stops—Etoile at the beginning of the avenue, Argentine in the middle, and Porte Maillot at the end. My stop was Argentine, two hundred feet from the entrance of our house. The whole avenue was lined with identical apartment houses, with very few stores except for flower shops, two bakeries, and several cafés. My favorite one was near the Etoile, and I often met my friends there, as I was afraid to bring them to the house. The shopping was on the side streets. Every day as I got out of the métro, I picked up the newspaper from the *kiosque* near my stop and then went to the bakery, Boulangerie Vaudois, and bought a baguette for dinner. Sometimes when I came home early I bought a small quiche and ate it before I went upstairs. My grandmother did not approve of eating between meals but I could not resist the smell of warm quiche. Between numbers 30 and 22 of Avenue de la Grande Armée was the American PX, where servicemen and their wives went shopping. My grandmother had befriended several of them because she spoke English well and also because right after the war the French were very thankful to the Americans for having helped to liberate Paris. At least once or twice a week an American was invited to dinner. As food was rationed, they often helped my grandmother by bringing coffee or butter or steaks to the house.

Rue des Acacias was our shopping street. There was the *crémerie,* where I went first to buy milk. After the war, you brought your metal pail to the *crémerie* and Mme Blanchette filled it up with milk using a large ladle. Butter, sold by the pound, was cut with a metal string from a *motte,* a hill of luscious, yellow creamy butter. I was always astounded that Mme Blanchette could cut exactly a pound if this is what you wanted. The butcher and the produce stores were next on my trip; first came the butcher. Meat was displayed in the window, laid out in an organized mosaic of reds and whites and yellows. The butcher's wife was a friend of my grandmother, who called ahead to order the meat for dinner. As I approached the end of the street I closed my eyes while passing the horse butcher. The store had a large gilded horse head outside above the large display window. I hated the store and hated horsemeat. If my grandmother asked me to buy some, I often came home empty-handed, feigning forgetfulness. The street ended at Place des Ternes. At the corner was Les Grands Magasins Réunis, a dowdy department store built in the early 1900s, and my grandmother's favorite shop. There she bought her amazing hats topped with birds or flowers and frumpy old-fashioned dresses ("everyday dresses," she called them). Unfortunately she bought my dresses there also, so I went around feeling out-of-fashion and unattractive. No argument would dissuade her. For the first year, the 17th arrondissement, my neighborhood, became my only world. When I returned after my wedding several years later, I was astonished at how nothing had changed.

My mother disappeared more and more often as the days went by. It was my grandmother who registered me at the Ecole de Jeunes Filles de Neuilly, a private school across from my brother's high school. I would have to be tutored all summer long, as my schooling at the Convent of the Sacred Heart had left me way behind most of the students my age.

A month after we arrived, my grandmother announced that we would all go to the sea. She chose Biarritz, but, it was my mother who rented and paid for the house. I would be tutored in the morning and my afternoons would be free to go to the beach and have fun. I thought my life was looking up.

3

*A Promise
Broken*

*A*s *long as you could* count your money, you were deemed good in math at the convent school in Cairo. Now I found myself ridiculed by my brother, Eddy, who tried to teach me the rudiments of algebra and geometry while we summered in a rented house by the sea. My grandmother chose Biarritz, where she had once owned a house during the years after World War I. I have a photograph of my grandmother at seventeen, lunching in the courtyard of that summer house, radiant among a dozen well-fed women dressed in white.

The large garden of this rented house had a grapevine-covered pergola where we had our meals. Eddy also tried to improve my spelling by giving me complex dictation. At lunch, he'd complain, "I can't teach her anything. She's a nitwit!" My mother would answer with a coy, feigned confusion, "I wonder why. Colette, did you know that Eddy was always excellent in math and that he learned to read when he was barely five?" I'd heard this since I was five myself, and had refused at first to learn how to read. Why was my brother so much brighter than me, I thought to myself.

Lunch was my salvation, as it interrupted the torture of my math lessons. We sat under the shaded pergola, drinking sparkling water with raspberry syrup or ice-cold lemonade. We often started with a salad of tomatoes, warm from the sun and sprinkled with fresh, whole tarragon leaves. Or we'd dig our knives into slabs of the local *pâté de campagne*. Georgette made a *friture,* tiny freshwater fish fried until crisp and tender, served with a bowl of coarse salt and potatoes sautéed in lard and tossed with fresh parsley. Dessert was always fruit: a bowl of dark red cherries or fragrant, juicy white peaches that my mother expertly peeled with a knife and fork.

In the afternoon we went swimming at the beach. Used to the warm waters of Alexandria, it took me awhile to brave the cold Atlantic and to walk barefoot over the stony shore. My mother lay on a chaise longue under a blue-and-white umbrella, reading a book or gossiping. Occasionally she'd go on a long walk down the beach with my brother. I found myself anticipating Georgette's consommé with marrow and the tender cold meats she served with Dijon mustard and a buttery green salad. Sometimes we drove to the local ice-cream shop or took in a film. I loved Gérard Philipe, the young actor who was the darling of all the young teenagers. My favorite movie was *Le Diable au Corps* (*Devil in the Flesh*), the story of a young man who falls in love with an older married woman and he has to give up their baby to her husband. It was a tragedy—the beautiful woman dying as she gave birth. I cried at the movie, which I must have seen at least four times.

While my mother was out dancing at the casinos, my grandmother and I chatted. Grandmaman did not approve of my dresses. They were too light, *trop ordinaire*, she said, shaking her head at my simple flower-print dress made by our local dressmaker in Cairo. "When we are back in Paris I will take you to my dressmaker. She will make you some dresses to wear on Sundays and when you go out; we can also buy some dresses to wear to school." My school had no uniform as the convent had. I said yes to everything Grandmaman suggested. I desperately wanted to please her so she would like me as much as she liked my brother. We went shopping together at Les Grands Magasins Réunis. In France at that time, dresses for children were by age. My grandmother was dismayed when I tried on the first dress she chose—a child's size 14. It was too small. "You must lose weight, Colette! You are too fat," she said with irritation. I was crushed. In the next few days every time my hand went for the bread on the table my grandmother gave me a stern look. I started to eat less so that I would lose weight and gain her approval.

Grandmaman was both my idol and my nemesis, a tall, very elegant, youthful, and horribly conceited woman of sixty-five.

As I walked down the street with her, men often turned around to stare at her small waist, copious breasts, and rounded hips. In the informal Biarritz streets, she donned large-brimmed hats decorated with flowers or birds. In Paris, her hats had veils that hid her face, so no one could see if she was old or young. Her hats amazed me. She never left the house without wearing one. *"J'ai une tête à chapeaux"* (I have a head for hats), she said proudly. I, too, have *"une tête à chapeaux"* and love to wear hats, but mine are a little more discreet. Her wavy hair was dyed a light chestnut and tied in the back in a loose chignon. A local Paris dressmaker made her dresses. She had been very rich before the war and had worn designer clothes. She could no longer afford them but had her entrée with many of the popular couturiers of the day. She would drag Mme Simone, her dressmaker, to the salons and have Mme S. copy the dresses she liked. I often lay on her bed on lazy mornings, watching Grandmaman dress. She asked me to help her lace up a corset with whalebone stays that made her stand majestically straight. She would slip a delicate blouse on and tuck it into a camel-hair skirt that fell to midcalf. She took a long time with her makeup, and while she applied it, she talked to me. "You must never wash your face with soap," she said, "very bad for your skin. Just use hot water, then a strong astringent to clean it. If you do that, you will never have wrinkles." I hung on her every word of advice, and I still don't use soap.

When she was ready, she walked purposefully to the kitchen

to have a conference with Georgette about the day's meals. On Saturday mornings, when I had a respite from the dreadful tutorial, I followed her to the market, lagging behind because she used a trot rather than a stroll, a wicker basket swinging furiously from her arm. In Cairo the market was an all-day affair. My Egyptian grandmother was a queen at the lavish outdoor market, greeted, saluted even, by name. In Biarritz we were the *summer people,* and were quite anonymous; still, by the third day Grandmaman had her favorite stands. Surrounding a large square, the stands displayed the best of French produce: white peaches piled high, perfumed melons, pears and yellow plums, pencil-thin *haricots verts,* Swiss chard, sorrel, and mounds of ruby red tomatoes, tiny onions, and at least five kinds of lettuce. I loved the smell of fresh sausages, pâtés, and boiled ham, the latter handed to me by the rotund *charcutière,* sliced paper-thin. Sometimes there was a whole roasted suckling pig. I begged Grandmaman to buy some for lunch and smiled at the saleslady, hoping she would add some of the crackling, roasted skin to my grandmother's order. The meat stand looked like a jewelry store, each roast beautifully wrapped in white fat, the lamb chops decorated with frilly crowns of paper. In Cairo, cheese was virtually unheard of; here in Biarritz, I slathered creamy Camembert on bread and greedily dipped my spoon into mounds of fresh, tangy farmer's cheese that Grandmaman bought from the *crémerie* at the market. Laden with all our purchases, we walked back to the car, stored the food, and Grandmaman turned to me and said gleefully,

"Une petite crêpe?" Hand in hand, we walked to the crêpe stand and shared a *crêpe Bretonne,* a thin, crispy buckwheat crêpe, sprinkled with sugar, butter, and lemon. At that moment life seemed perfect to me.

The days passed very quickly but on our last night in Biarritz, my world collapsed. We were sitting in the garden. For once my mother stayed with us, and as we watched the evening sun light up the sky with fiery oranges and pinks before it disappeared, she said in a matter-of-fact voice, "I think I will go back to Egypt next week." Just like that. I was dumbfounded. Nobody said a word, and I felt my own throat tighten. She haɑ promised to stay . . . how could she leave me again? I looked first at my brother, who was stoically resting his chin on his fists, and then at my grandmother, who looked strangely pleased. They each caught the other's eye, and they smiled. I understood. My mother had come between her and my brother. If she left, my grandmother would have Eddy and me to herself! I got up and walked away, rage overwhelming my young heart. "I hate her," I muttered to myself. "She never keeps her promises. Why did I think she would? I wish she had left me in Cairo." Suddenly my mother was beside me, murmuring soothing words like "I will come back, I promise . . . it's only for a few months . . . don't be angry . . . you get along with Rose . . . you'll be happy." I walked quickly out of her reach and to my bed to weep.

*   *   *

Back in Paris, the next weeks passed very quickly. My mother was never home, always shopping for her friends and for herself. A coat for Lola, my young godmother, presents for her friend Elie, things for herself. Nothing for me. I was jealous of the time she spent shopping for others. I went shopping with my grandmother. Dresses to go to school, navy blue with a white collar, and elegant dresses for Sunday dinners or to go out. "The child needs a coat," my grandmother said to my mother. "Then buy her one," she answered. There were long discussions about money. I eavesdropped and gradually began to understand what was going on. I learned that my father had left a will leaving my mother lots of money but also dividing the rest of his fortune between my brother and me. My uncle Clément, my father's younger brother, was our guardian. My grandmother was being paid a monthly stipend to take care of us. I heard my mother say, "You will have enough money for both. If not let me know; I will talk to Clément." I realized that all the things my grandmother was buying me as gifts were in fact paid for by me. I felt betrayed by all of them. No one had cared enough to explain things to me. The day my mother left, I cried myself to sleep. She had said goodbye, and again promised to come back in three months. She returned four years later.

Once my mother was gone, my grandmother decided that I should move to the front bedroom, which had been occupied by my mother. The room was very large with two French windows overlooking the avenue. If I opened the French doors and stood on the narrow balcony, I could get a glimpse of the Arc de Triomphe. The room had a fireplace with a coal stove, as the apartment was not yet centrally heated. (In the winter we had to go to the basement and carry up the coal, which was in the cellar. I always froze in that room. I used to put my clothes under the mattress so they would be warm when I got up.) Above the mantelpiece was a very large gilded mirror. Between the two windows stood a heavy, inlaid mahogany dresser. A double bed (called *un lit matrimonial*) was set in an alcove covered with a blue canopy. The wall behind the bed was draped with blue silk, and the bed board was upholstered in the same fabric. A blue silk comforter was spread across the bed. The room was lit with a crystal chandelier, very similar to the one in the living room. An Oriental rug with blue overtones covered half the parquet floor. This had been my grandmother's room when my grandfather was alive, and it was beautiful. At fifteen, however, I felt totally estranged from it. It would never be mine even after five years. I hated the room as much as I hated my life.

I had an additional problem now. My grandmother's attitude toward me had changed since my mother left us. She was abrupt with me and often quite sarcastic. Stories about the war were told to me at every turn. Did I know that my brother had to wear the yellow Jewish star while I was frolicking in Cairo? (I learned later that he only had to wear it the last few months of the war, as no one knew that my grandparents were Jewish. Furthermore, my brother had an Egyptian passport, which the Germans respected, since King Farouk was secretly their ally.)

Had I heard about the six million Jews who had died in concentration camps? She pushed guilt on me as if it were her daily chore, and I was enraged by the injustice. I was six years old when the war broke out; how could I know anything? Could I have done something for the Jews? Was I a Jew myself? I no longer knew where I belonged, who or what I was. I tried to push the convent, with its peace and incense and civil rules, away from my psyche, and I tried to sound Jewish, to feel Jewish. I never quite succeeded. I often complained to Georgette, who would kiss me and soothe me with her wonderful *pain perdu* (French toast made with slices of stale baguette and sprinkled with sugar) while I was sitting down at the table in the kitchen doing my homework. One day, when my grand-

Georgette's Pain Perdu

Georgette made French toast with leftover brioche bread. It can be made with any day-old bread but tastes much better with brioche. Cut 6 slices of day-old brioche about 1½ inches thick. In a microwave heat 3 cups of milk with ¼ teaspoon vanilla. Pour the hot milk over the brioche. Allow the bread to soak up the milk. In a bowl beat 2 eggs with a fork. In a large skillet melt 2 tablespoons butter with 2 tablespoons oil. When the oil is hot, dip the slices in the egg and sauté until they are golden. Serve with powdered sugar. Serves 6.

mother had refused to let me go to a friend's house, I ran into the kitchen crying, "I hate her! She is so horrible; she dislikes me and only likes Eddy. He can go where he pleases and do what he pleases!" Georgette looked at me and said in a sad voice, "Let me explain to you what happened. A few weeks ago, we removed the sheets in the room you first slept in and turned over the mattress; she found your missal. She was very upset. Someone had told her that your mother converted to Catholicism, but she did not know about you. She is very angry." I was astonished; why had she not asked me? Why had she not said anything to me? I could not understand. I was furious at my mother for lying to me and to her mother. My Egyptian grandparents had known about my conversion but had acted kindly toward me. I decided not to say anything to my grandmother and tried to do exactly what she wanted. Georgette had told me that before and during the war, my grandparents never openly said they were Jewish. My grandfather had changed his name to Bémant, which was not a Jewish name. For this reason, during the occupation they had been left alone. But now my grandmother had decided to become more religious, but only for the High Holidays. She would take us to temple for Passover. At night I'd say a small prayer to the Virgin Mary, asking for forgiveness for having abandoned what I thought was my religion.

To please my grandmother, I offered to help her in the kitchen. Ironically, this was the only place where we seemed to get along. In the kitchen my grandmother was pleasant and talkative. She wasn't a great cook but there were a few dishes that she prepared very well. She was famous for her stuffed carp, and I dutifully sat in the kitchen, peeling carrots, onions, shallots, and garlic. She sliced the carp with a large butcher knife. Often she asked me to hold the fish while she banged on the knife with a hammer while I tightly closed my eyes. I did not like the slimy feeling the fish skin gave me. "The center bone is very tough," she explained while she delicately removed the fish flesh with a sharp knife, careful not to cut the skin. I talked to her about my best friend, Claudine, the only one of my friends she liked and accepted. In the winter she made a stuffed goose that was superb. The best part of that dish was the neck; my job was to sew the neck skin with a long needle and black thread to end up with a long pocket. She stuffed the neck with the goose liver, onions, and sausage. The neck was roasted alongside the goose and eaten cold, sliced and dabbed with mustard. I loved that dish and make it at least once a year. Another one of her signature dishes was her meat loaf, a mixture of pork, veal, and beef. She placed a row of hard-boiled eggs inside the forcemeat, and when served, each slice had a sun in its center. At Christmastime, she and I would prepare four-meat pâtés to give to her non-Jewish friends and to my uncle Clément. I've kept up this tradition through all these years, and every December, my children and I make pâtés as gifts. These moments with my grandmother were rare, however; most of the time, we argued bitterly. She had developed a new technique to deal with me. Everytime I wanted to go out with my friends on

Roast Goose with Stuffed Neck

The day before, wipe the goose (about 8 to 10 pounds) inside and out with paper towels. Remove as much fat as possible. Set aside the heart and the liver. Stuff the goose with paper towels and refrigerate, uncovered, overnight. Meanwhile, spread the neck skin on the countertop, remove all veins, and sew the skin so as to have a large tube. Leave a small opening. In a bowl mix together the liver and the heart, each cut into bite-size pieces, the goose fat, cut into small pieces, 2 Italian sausages, casing removed, 1 egg, and 3 tablespoons flour. Add salt and pepper to taste and 1 tablespoon chopped sage. Mix all the ingredients together and stuff the neck. Close the opening and refrigerate until ready to bake. The next day, remove the paper towels from the goose's cavity and prick the skin all over with a fork. Peel 2 garlic cloves, cut them into slivers, and insert them into the goose flesh. Rub the goose with coarse salt and sprinkle with freshly ground pepper. Place the goose on a rack in a pan and next to it the stuffed neck. Add 2 cups water to the pan and bake in a preheated 325-degree oven for 4 hours, basting from time to time. Halfway through the cooking, remove all the fat to a bowl. Add 2 more cups water to the pan and continue baking until the juice from the thigh runs clear when pierced with a fork. Remove the goose from the oven and allow to

*stand at room temperature for 15 minutes
before carving. Wrap the cool neck in foil and
refrigerate overnight. The next day thinly slice
the neck and serve with Dijon mustard and a
green salad for lunch.* Serves 8.

the weekend, she had *une crise cardiaque* (a heart attack) and I
had to cancel my date. If I invited friends over, her heart attack
reoccurred and she told my friends that I did not care if she
died. My friends started to refuse to come to our house, except
Claudine. But even Claudine did not come very often, needing
to keep her mother company. My brother was no help, as he was
busy with his studies and his girlfriend. I wrote my mother that
I wanted to go home. My mother answered a month later, asking me to have patience; it could not be so terrible. I spoke to
my uncle, whose favorite answer to anything was, "Here is two
hundred francs; buy yourself a nice dress." This time he added,
"Une jeune fille de bonne famille reste à la maison avec sa famille"
(A well-brought up girl stays at home.). "But it is my money," I
cried in anger, but my uncle patted my head and said, "Have
patience; it is only for a few more years." There was no one to
help me or advise me on what to do except Georgette.

Georgette's kitchen was my haven. Back from school at four,
I would sit at the enamel table, push away the *toile ciré,* and
start my homework while Georgette made me a buttered *tartine*
with thin slices of *saucisson à l'ail* (garlic sausage). Sometimes,

Meat Loaf

In a large bowl mix together 1 pound chopped veal and 1 pound chopped pork. Add 1 pound chopped beef. Add 1 egg and mix well. In a skillet heat 2 tablespoons butter, add 2 small onions, chopped, and sauté until transparent. Add the onion to the chopped meat along with salt and pepper to taste, 1 tablespoon thyme, and 1 tablespoon chopped sage. Mix well; if the meat is too loose add ½ cup breadcrumbs. Mix well. Form the meat into 2 long loaves. Open the center of each loaf and place in each 4 hard-boiled eggs end-to-end. Enclose the eggs with the meat. Peel 3 garlic cloves, cut them into slivers, and insert them into the meat. Place the loaves in a baking pan. Cover the top of each loaf with 2 slices of bacon. Add 1½ cups chicken stock to the pan. Bake in a preheated 350-degree oven for 1 hour. Remove from the oven and allow to cool. If the meat loaves are to be served cold, wrap in foil and refrigerate overnight. Refrigerate the pan juices. The next day, remove the layer of fat from the juices and slice the jelly. Thinly slice the meat, garnish with the jelly, and serve with Dijon mustard. If the loaves are to be served hot, slice the meat, cover with the pan juices, and serve. Serves 6.

she plied me with petits fours that she had bought just for me
at the pâtisserie round the corner and hid behind some jam jars
in the pantry. She did not want my grandmother—who commanded me to stay slim—to see them. While I worked she
talked about her life with my grandparents. She had come to
their house when she was barely seventeen as a *femme de chambre* (a personal maid) for my grandmother. Grandmaman
trained her to serve at her fancy dinners, and later on pushed
her to learn how to cook. She loved my grandfather, who had
given her books to read and sent her to school to get her *certificat d'études* (high school equivalency) so that she could get a
better job. She told me once that one of my grandfather's
friends, an older gentleman and a widower, had proposed to
her. My grandfather had urged her to marry him, but my
grandmother had put a stop to it, telling Georgette she would
be miserable because her low social background would make it
impossible for her to fit into her suitor's world. As she was
telling me the story, I saw in her eyes that to this day she regret-
ted her decision. During the war, Georgette wanted to leave
and join her family but she stayed with my grandparents
because of my grandfather. Often when things got tough and
food was scarce, she bicycled to her family farm to get some
ham or potatoes or vegetables to bring back to my family. And
then my grandfather became very ill. "He was dying, Colette,"
she told me, tears in her eyes, "and Mme Rose, she wasn't very
nice to him. So I took care of him." Georgette would wipe her
eyes and start cooking. She sautéed cubes of smoked lard for a

white bean soup or, knowing how much I loved chestnuts, made braised veal with chestnuts, or a *gâteau de marrons* (chestnut cake) for the weekend. People in the building often came to see her to discuss their problems, mainly of the heart. Mlle Blanchard, the dressmaker on the third floor rear, was a frequent visitor. She had been engaged to the same man for the last ten years but he seemed never to want to marry her. "You know, Georgette," she'd say, "I love him, but I am not getting younger. He is scared of marriage, and I don't know what to do," and she'd burst into tears. Each time Georgette would pat her back and try to convince her to leave him and go out with other men. Mlle Blanchard would nod her head, say that Georgette was right, and then a few days later go back to her fiancé. Then there was the couple on the second floor with a small baby. The husband had lost his job, was drinking, and quite regularly beat his wife. The wife would come running to Georgette, hand her the baby, and say, "I am going to my mother; I will be back in a few hours to take him there." She'd come back, take the baby, and say in a meek voice, "My mother thinks I should try to make peace with him. You see, he is very upset because he has no job." "That is why, Colette," Georgette would say, sighing, "I never married. Men are not to be trusted!" I would think of my Egyptian grandfather, who loved my grandmother so much. He was kind to everyone. *I will,* I thought, *find a man like him!* When I was very upset about something my grandmother had said or done, Georgette hugged me and said, "Don't worry . . . when you are eighteen you can leave. You are strong and intelligent. Don't fight back right now." I took her advice and bided my time.

From time to time, on Sundays my grandmother invited her friends for lunch. There was a lawyer, Pierre, who came often to the house. He always paid me a compliment. Sometimes he'd bring me a present—a silver bracelet, a ribbon for my hair, tickets for the Comédie Française. He asked me where I went to school, what time I got out, did I enjoy my courses . . . One day I saw his car in front of my school. "Jump in, Colette. I was just passing by and I remember you went to school here. I will drive you home." I had just been reading *Claudine à l'Ecole,* Colette's first novel, and I thought, *How great! I am having the same adventure!* Driving me home, Pierre asked if I would like to have my own apartment and stay with him. I looked at him. He had hair coming out of his nose, and his hands, with their long, gnarled fingers, looked like eagle's claws. Fear and disgust gripped me. I said, "No, thank you" in a tight, hoarse voice, and as he stopped in front of the house, he whispered in my ear, "Don't tell Rose!"

I ran to Georgette and immediately told her what happened. Georgette sat down with me and said in a low voice, "You know, Colette, older men are like this. . . . You are very sexy; you have such lovely eyes, and often you laughed when he complimented you. And also remember, you accepted his gifts. He thought you understood. Don't worry; it will never happen again." I looked at Georgette's big, expressive eyes. Everyone agreed that she was a beauty. For the first time I asked myself if she had had the same adventures. Did she have a boyfriend? I did not feel at that moment I could ask. "I want to have adventures, Georgette. I wanted someone to tell me I was beautiful, sexy, but not Pierre! I don't like him. I want to meet someone but he has to be young and charming." No young men had ever whistled as I passed by, no boys had ever waited for me at the corner. I suddenly felt sad. Did I appeal only to old men? I asked Georgette. She laughed and said, "Just wait . . . you'll see."

She made me a cup of hot chocolate and then went to find my grandmother to tell her. My grandmother came to the kitchen and said in an angry voice, "These are tales, lies . . . he would never do that. You read too many cheap novels. Pierre is an old friend." She had not believed me. I was crushed but Pierre never came again to the house.

I got my answer about Georgette's private life six months later and this event shattered my life. Georgette announced that she was leaving. She had found a job in a factory and was also getting married to the foreman. I cried and begged her not to leave me with that horrible woman. Georgette embraced me and said, "You will be my bridesmaid and will come to see me often." The wedding was a small affair. They were married at City Hall in a simple, brief ceremony. There was a small lunch at the local restaurant paid for by my grandmother. I saw Georgette once or twice in the following six months.

The last time I saw her was in the hospital. Georgette was lying in a bed looking thin and tired. She was dying of cancer. I sat down next to her and started to cry. Georgette took my hand and squeezed it hard. "Don't cry, Colette," she said in a small, wispy voice "You'll be all right " How could I be all right when there was no one left I could talk to? She was the only one, like Ahmet in Cairo, who had taken me in. She had opened her heart to a lonely girl. She also allowed me to help her in the kitchen. And because of her, I found out that I loved to cook. We would gossip together about my grandmother, the people in the courtyard, and what was happening to me in school. I realized, sitting there, that I had never asked her any personal questions, never asked her how she was or whether she was happy. My voice broke as my heart poured out to her. "Georgette, I am so sorry, I am so sorry . . . I love you so much and I miss you." Georgette again squeezed my hand and said, "I love you too." A nurse came in and said I had to leave right away. Georgette was tired and needed rest. I bent down and kissed her. "I will be back soon." But she died only days later. Once again, I thought I must be cursed. All the people I love leave me or die!

4

Student Life,
Saucisson Sec,
and Swimming
Pools

*M*any *of the lycées,* or public secondary schools, in Paris were closed down at the time my grandmother was considering where to place me for my new French education. During the war, the school buildings had been occupied by the Gestapo or used as headquarters for the German army brass and thus were in serious need of refurbishment. Although normally I would have attended the Lycée La Fontaine (my own neighborhood lycée), my grandmother and my uncle Clément agreed that it would be safer for me to travel by métro to L'Ecole de Jeunes Filles de Neuilly, a private school for upper-middle-class families located in a town house in an elegant suburb. My brother's lycée was just across the street and he could keep an eye on me. We had a long walk from the métro stop to the school, but my brother kept his silence as usual. On my first day, fear compelled me to ask him to accompany me to the door. What if the kids did not like me? What if they made fun of my singsong Egyptian accent? Eddy, in a moment of empathy, told me that my accent was all right, that it had improved since the day we arrived, and that he was sure there would be lots of new students. He walked with me to the school door and introduced me to the teacher in charge of greeting the students. In front of the school gate was a small plaza where all the students gathered. I stared. Although there was no uniform or even dress code at lycées, everyone seemed to wear the same sort of outfit here: a navy blue dress with a white collar or a navy blue skirt with a white blouse. My grandmother had dressed me just as they were, yet I felt foreign and different. Most of the students had long, straight blond or chestnut hair and were very thin or at least seemed so to me. I was self-conscious of my tawny skin, large breasts, and round hips. In Egypt I would have been considered lovely and sexy; here, I felt like an elephant. But when I look at pictures of myself at that age, I realize that I was not fat, nor did my breasts really stick out as I felt they did that day. I was fifteen years old, awkward, and not at all sophisticated. A bell rang and we were told to line up by class. I found myself standing near a girl of about my height with curly brown hair. Right away I thought she could be my friend; she did not look much different from me. "My name is Colette, what's yours?" I said shyly. "Claudine," she responded, smiling. "You know, it's funny how you are Colette and Colette the writer wrote many books about Claudine, I am new here, are you?" As I nodded yes, she added, "Then we can be friends." This first exchange would seal a friendship that still exists today.

Every morning my brother and I went together to school but in the late afternoon I went home with my friends. I sat in class near Claudine. On the other side sat Nicole, a short, round girl whose mother had died when she was very young. Her brother, who was much older than she, brought her up. The three of us were inseparable. Later during the school year I found out that both Claudine and Nicole were Jewish, as was my third friend Judith, whose father was a prominent lawyer. After class we would walk together to the métro. The four of us had problems at home that were similar but somewhat different. My father was dead, I was abandoned by my mother, and I did not get along with my grandmother; Nicole had lost her mother, and her father did not take care of her; Judith belonged to an enormous family of eight brothers and sisters and felt lost and overlooked in the crowd. Claudine's story, we knew, was more dramatic. Her father had been a minister in Léon Blum's government just as the war had broken out. When the Nazis occupied Paris, her father was imprisoned but he made a deal with the Germans, agreeing to be sent to a concentration camp if they left his family alone. A deal was struck and he was sent away, never to come back. He left behind four daughters and one son. Claudine was just six years old but her brother and sisters were much older. As the war progressed the son joined the Resistance, was caught, and shot. The older sister committed suicide and the other sisters worked for the Resistance until the war was over. Heartbroken, Claudine's mother withdrew to her bedroom in the enormous house they lived in and locked herself away with her books. Claudine, left to fend for herself, was taken care of by Alice, their housekeeper, who had spent her life with the family. The four of us were very good students. I was good in history, Claudine in English, Nicole was the math one, and Judith was the best writer. We helped one another with our homework at each other's house.

On our first day of school, the homeroom teacher read the names of all the students out loud. My grandmother had made the mistake of registering me with my full name. There were about four Colettes in my class, so the teacher announced that we would be called by our last names, but first she said she would call the students by their full names so that she could be sure we were in the right class. When it came to my name, I blushed with embarrassment when I heard her say Colette Sol Palacci. All the girls burst out laughing. In the few weeks that followed they improvised, which doesn't quite translate in English, a song with my name: *"Mlle Sol habite à l'entre-sol, où elle mange une sole en chantant d'une voix fausse: Do Re Mi Fa Sol."* The teacher heard it and interrupted the girls, explaining that I came from Egypt and that it was my first time in France and in a French school. They stopped singing that song when they saw me, but I was given the nickname "l'Egyptienne," which I hated, as I wanted above all to be French. To my chagrin, during the two years I went to that school my nickname stuck, although by the end of the year I had nearly lost my Egyptian accent and my suntan.

I was a good student except in math. I loved to memorize poems and often volunteered to recite them in a loud, dramatic voice, especially Victor Hugo's works. My friends Claudine, Nicole, and Judith made fun of me but I knew I was good and that our teacher, Mlle Renaud, liked my recitation. The first three months, life was a simple routine. Morning in school, lunch at home, school again in the afternoon, then a slow walk back with my new friends to the métro entrance. We all stopped on the way at a *boulangerie-pâtisserie.* My friends bought *petit pains au chocolat* but I disliked the sweet croissant stuffed with a bar of chocolate. Instead, I bought a *ficelle,* a very thin baguette that is more crust than anything else. I ate it all in the time it took us to walk from the *boulangerie* to the métro. My friends teased me, *"Tu es une paysanne . . . tu manges du pain pour ton goûter!"* (You are a peasant . . . you eat bread for your snack!) In the days that followed I decided that I too should find something to eat more in keeping with French tradition. I looked around for something savory and discovered the bakery's twisted cheese sticks made of flaky pastry. They were thin, crisp, and slightly spicy. And to my friends' delight, from that day on, every afternoon I ate at least two.

Weekends were more difficult. My friends were too new, and I did not dare ask what they were doing on weekends. Also, both Claudine and Judith didn't come to class on Saturday morning as the rest of us did. I was confused and asked my brother. "They are Jewish and probably religious," he said. I wanted to tell them that I was both Jewish and Catholic but felt they wouldn't understand and decided to say nothing. My grandmother insisted that my brother take me around the Champs Elysées, down the Place de la Concorde, to the Tuileries Gardens, and back home for lunch. We were both bored with each other, and I was yearning to roam around Paris unfettered, but I did not dare ask. Lunch on Sunday was another ordeal. We always went to the same restaurant near the house and had the same pedestrian leg of lamb and the same dessert (one that I detested)—ice-cream cake. If I suggested the fish of the day or berries with cream, my grandmother frowned and said in a pinched voice, *"Cet enfant n'a aucun goût. Elle est vraiment une Egyptienne!"* (This child has no taste. She really is an Egyptian!) Once in a while Uncle Clément, my guardian, took us out to lunch. He was the only one of my grandfather's eight children who had not been brought up in Egypt. At the age of ten, he had contracted an eye disease that many Egyptian children had. In the fall, a wind called Hamsin blew sand from the desert into the cities and countryside. Grains of sand lodged under a child's eyelid and infection set in. In the poor countryside, the child eventually went blind. Clément was luckier. He was sent off to Paris to be cured and cared for by several aunts, and he stayed the rest of his days. Despite the distance between them, Clément kept in close contact with his siblings and supported them when they came to Paris to study. A successful architect, he served a mostly Egyptian clientele who were interested in investing their money in Parisian real estate, sensing that a revolution and a change in the regime were not far off.

Clément was short with wavy black hair and round glasses. He drove around Paris in a spiffy sports car and loved good food and fun. I was intrigued by his little secret, which I found out about soon after arriving in Paris. As I understood it, when my father met my mother, he had a mistress named Germaine, tall, sexy, and direct. My father broke up with her when he got engaged to my mother, and Germaine was *passed on* to his brother. My father made Clément swear that he would never marry her. Clément kept his promise and lived with her in a beautiful apartment in a building he himself designed, near the Bois de Boulogne. When we went out, Germaine never accompanied us. My aunts, uncles, and cousins disliked her and often talked about her disparagingly. Clément, who was kind, protected her from all of them and kept her away.

I adored my uncle, who tried hard to help me but because he had had no children, did not understand why I was so unhappy. He was conservative and thought that women should stay home and get married. I loved going out with him and couldn't wait until the next time he took us to lunch. He was fond of good food, and we inspired each other as we explored neighborhood bistros to hunt down the best seasonal dishes. There was one that I liked more than the others—Café Allard on the Left Bank—that served a scrumptious rabbit stewed in wine with mushrooms and a wickedly rich potato gratin alongside. (I often make this dish for

Rabbit with Prunes and Raisins

The day before, place the liver of a 3- to 4-pound rabbit in a bowl and cover with 1½ cups red wine. Cut the rabbit into serving pieces and place them in a large salad bowl. Add 4 tablespoons olive oil, 4 cups red wine, and ¼ cup red wine vinegar. Add 2 thyme sprigs, 1 bay leaf, 2 parsley sprigs, a teaspoon of crushed black pepper, and 4 juniper berries and refrigerate. Turn the rabbit several times. The next day, dice 5 slices of lean bacon. Remove the rabbit from the marinade, reserving it, dry the rabbit with paper towels, and dust with flour. In a large saucepan heat 2 tablespoons olive oil. Add the rabbit pieces and brown on all sides for about 8 minutes. Remove the rabbit from the pan and drain the fat. In the same saucepan heat 2 tablespoons butter and add 4 shallots, peeled and chopped, and the bacon. Cook for 4 minutes. Add the rabbit pieces. Strain the marinade through a fine sieve and add half to the saucepan. Cover and simmer for 1 hour. After 25 minutes of cooking, add 2 cups pitted prunes and ¼ cup raisins. Add more marinade, if necessary. The rabbit should be barely covered. Ten minutes before the end of the cooking time, add the liver. Correct the seasoning with salt and pepper. Serve with steamed small potatoes. Serves 4.

friends but today I add fresh chestnuts and Chinese dried mush-rooms to the stew.) When I went out with Clément I could choose any dessert I wanted. In the spring, I invariably chose berries with thick crème fraîche. When I got home, I described each dish to Georgette, who promised to make me the same gratin. But she never did. Grandmaman objected to it, saying that the dish was fattening and that I should be careful with my weight. "You're Egyptian, remember? They all get fat!" Ashamed, I'd promise myself that the next time I went out with Clément I would be very careful not to choose something fattening. I could never keep my promise.

Potatoes in Cream au Gratin

Preheat the oven to 345 degrees. Peel 5 very large potatoes. For this dish I like to use Idaho potatoes. Thinly slice the potatoes and place in a bowl. Cover with ice water to prevent the potatoes from getting brown. Butter a gratin dish. Drain the potatoes and dry them with paper towels. Cover the bottom of the dish with a layer of potatoes. Sprinkle with salt and pepper and thin slices of onion and dot with ½ tablespoon butter. Repeat this step until all the potatoes have been used. In a small bowl beat 1 egg with ½ cup cream. Pour the cream over the potatoes. Top the potatoes with 4 thin slices of Gruyère. Reduce the heat to 325 degrees and bake for 45 minutes, or until the top is brown and the potatoes are tender. Serve in the baking dish. Serves 4.

* * *

A few months after I had settled into my routine, I made another discovery, one that influenced my future. I took the métro every morning at Porte Maillot, about two blocks from my grandmother's apartment. One particularly sleepy morning, I got out by mistake at the Pont de Neuilly and to my surprise found myself at the beginning of a farmers' market. Not wanting to return to the métro, I started walking through the market, which happens to be one of the longest in Paris—over ten blocks. It was early October, and I could not belie ʾe my eyes. The market was more beautiful and smelled better t ıan the one I used to love in Cairo—garlic piled high or braided, knobby globes of celery root, glossy chestnuts, muscat grapes, rosy apples, pomegranates. I wanted to try them all! What really ignited my passion, though, were the charcuterie stands. The smell of smoked ham and salamis was more than I could bear. I bought 100 grams of *saucisson sec* (hard salami), 100 grams of *jambon de Bayonne* (a sort of French prosciutto), and was about to buy more when I realized that I was on my way to school. When and how was I going to eat all of this? But the next stand had all sorts of artisanal breads, so I bought two rolls and decided that I would skip my first class and sit on a bench to eat my treasures. This was the beginning of a long-lived habit I had of skipping a class from time to time to escape the drudgery of my life and to find solace in things I loved to do, namely looking at food and eating it. After my early lunch, I continued to stroll and discovered an array of stands selling salads that I had never seen—bright green mâche, tender, pale yellow frisée, Batavia, and watercress. The olive stand soon became a favorite of mine. Ibrahim, an Algerian immigrant who ran it, was in his late twenties, with black curly hair that fell over his forehead, large black eyes, and a very warm smile. He came to Paris when he was ten years old. His father was an olive merchant in Algeria before the war so Ibrahim continued his father's trade in Paris, selling olives and pickles at different markets around the city. In the months ahead we became very good friends, and every Wednesday I would stop at the market, walk to his stand, and choose a different kind of olive. He always had a pita bread ready for me and he stuffed it with feta cheese and olives. It was my favorite moment of the week! (A year ago I went back to the Neuilly market and found out that Ibrahim's grandson was now selling the olives.) I stared at the chickens, neatly plucked and labeled, rabbits, roasts, fish, and seafood. I'd whisper to Georgette about what I had seen. "Why must we have *colin* (hake)?" I whined. "It's so bland. Can't we have the fish I've seen in the market?" Georgette explained that my tightfisted grandmother thought they were too expensive. "Next time your uncle takes you out to lunch, ask for sole or *turbotin.*" I followed her advice, but the fish was always smothered in butter or cream, not the way I imagined it should be prepared. I began to ask for my sole to be grilled, which delighted my uncle. My love of markets has stayed with me, and my travels have led me to magnificent farmers' markets around the world.

*   *   *

When Georgette got married and left my grandmother's employ, I lost the only friend and ally I had in that house. Right after that, a revolution in Egypt sent shock waves through my North African family's lives. Colonel Nasser took over and King Farouk was sent into exile, as were all my uncles, aunts, and cousins, who fled to France or South America. My grandfather, who did not believe that the revolutionary government would consider him a foreigner, was heartbroken when they took over his business. He became sick, stayed in bed, and as my grandmother wrote me later, died in the spring. My cousins and uncles wanted my grandmother to come back to Paris with them but she refused to go. She died soon after. All my ties to Egypt and to my childhood were broken forever. I was overwhelmed by loneliness and a persistent feeling of being detached from my roots, from anything stable. Even my own mother, who wrote that she was finally coming home, decided to find herself a studio in Paris where she would live alone. To assuage my depression, I daydreamed of how I'd convince her to let me live with her. I awaited her arrival with a mixture of dread and excitement.

A month later, the new Egyptian government blocked my bank account and allowed only a certain sum to be used for my living expenses and my schooling. It was decided, against my pleas, that I should attend a regular lycée. I'd have to leave my friends and the teachers I knew and liked. I knew that my friend Claudine would be the only one with whom I could keep in touch.

Lycée La Fontaine was located in Auteuil, about half an hour from our house. It was a very modern school, the only one built just before the war, with science labs, elevators, and an enormous gym. The six-story building stood near a large park and an enclosed public swimming pool, *la piscine Molitor.* Although at first I was certain that I'd be lost among its thousands of students, I became known rather quickly. It started with the swimming pool. In Egypt, swimming had been part of my daily life because of the heat. I was proud of being a good swimmer, and when I first returned to Paris, I missed swimming in a pool. But now I could get my swimming in, which I did once or twice a week on my way to school. Sliding into the cool water and feeling it glide over my head made me feel free, like a mermaid. It was also the only sport I was good at. I would get to school with wet hair, quite frazzled because I had to run to get to class on time. Sometimes I didn't make it and I would have to come up with a plausible story: my bicycle broke down, I had a flat tire, my grandmother was sick, the buses were on strike. After a while, my stories became more elaborate, and rather macabre accidents were numerous, as well as bomb scares and helping blind men or crippled women to their houses, arms straining with their groceries. History was my first class of the day, and M. Ribaud would stop the class as I entered his room sheepishly and ask, in an imperious tone, "So Mlle Palacci, who did you save this morning?" My classmates laughed as I tried to think up a believable story. I usually failed but I was a good history student, and he never punished me. However, my reputation preceded me, and over the next two years I got into trouble at every turn. I often received *zéro de conduite* (zero for behavior), and once every two or three months was sent home for a day or two. I used that time to roam the city and swim. My grandmother was never quite aware of what was happening, since I made sure to leave the house at the same time every morning.

Lunch was another challenge. Now that I was attending the lycée, I had to have lunch near the school so I could be on time for my afternoon classes. My friends and I frequented a café near the school where the most popular quick meal was a *sandwich au jambon*, a piece of crusty baguette, split and slathered with butter and a couple of slices of ham. It didn't satisfy me— too much butter or not enough, ham too thick or too thin. I then switched to a *croque-monsieur*, two slices of bread stuffed with Swiss cheese and a slice of ham, sautéed in a skillet until golden brown. Still, not quite right. Tentatively, I began to explore the neighborhood with Brigitte, one of my friends who, like me, liked to eat. We found the Café Laure on the Rue de Lonchamps, run by a young woman who had lost her husband during the war. Mme Laure was Marseillaise and very quickly adopted Brigitte and me. Our ham sandwich was filled with a light *pistou*, a dark green sauce made with parsley and herbs, redolent of garlic. Sometimes we switched to her egg tart with tomatoes, hot peppers, and olives. Soon half of the lycée learned of our discovery, and Mme Laure's café was full all day

Tarte à la Tomate

Make the tart dough. In the bowl of a food processor place ½ cup chilled butter, cut into small pieces, along with 3 tablespoons vegetable shortening. Process for 1 minute and add 2 cups flour and ½ teaspoon salt. Process for 3 minutes and add 6 tablespoons ice water. Process until the dough forms a ball. Remove the dough from the work bowl, wrap it in foil, and refrigerate for 2 to 3 hours. Remove the dough from the refrigerator and bring it to room temperature. Butter a 9-inch tart pan. On a floured board roll the dough from the center out to form a circle. Line the tart pan with the dough, crimp the edges, and with a fork prick the bottom. Line the pie dough with 6 slices of Gruyère and bake the pie in a preheated 350-degree oven for 15 minutes. Remove from the oven and set aside. Place 4 large tomatoes in a large bowl, cover with boiling water, and let the tomatoes stand in the water for 3 minutes. Drain and refresh under cold running water. Peel the tomatoes, slice them, and remove the seeds. Sprinkle the slices with salt and leave them in a bowl for 15 minutes. Drain the tomatoes. In a food processor or blender finely chop ¼ cup fresh basil leaves with 1 tablespoon fresh thyme, salt and pepper, 1 garlic clove, and 2 tablespoons olive oil. Arrange the tomato slices in

concentric circles on top of the Gruyère.
Sprinkle with the basil mixture and bake for
another 10 minutes, or until the edges are
golden brown. Serve with a green salad.
Serves 4.

long. Brigitte and I became guests of honor and never had to
pay for more than our drinks.

My social life outside of school was dismal. Since Georgette
had left us, my grandmother did the cooking, and every week
she served us the same dishes. I grudgingly helped in the
kitchen, washed the dishes, and made my bed. We had a *femme
de ménage,* a cleaning woman, who came every other day. I
never even considered inviting my friends over, petrified that
my grandmother would have one of her simulated heart attacks
or start screaming at me in front of them. Most every time I was
invited out she'd have another heart attack, or I'd be too afraid
to leave her in case her attack was real. If I did leave, I'd worry.
At that time, French girls did not go out with boys on dates. We
went in a group to the movies, or to one another's homes for
parties. Of course, I was never allowed to host. My grandmother
rarely talked to me and my brother was never home. Life in that
enormous apartment was often grim, loveless, and cold.

*　*　*

Six months later my mother returned to Paris. One of her friends had found her an apartment, but my mother did not want me there on the grounds that I'd be better taken care of by my grandmother. I wept, yelled, and pleaded but to no avail. She mentioned, as a final argument, that my guardian had made the decision. I immediately called my uncle Clément. What were his reasons for wanting me to stay where I did not want to be, with a woman who hated me? After the first few words I heard—ones that I had grown to despise (*une jeune fille de bonne famille ne fait pas . . .*)—I knew there was nothing I could do. I had to stay! Years later, on one of my trips to Paris, I asked Clément why he had insisted that I stay with my grandmother. He stoically answered, "I was afraid your mother would let you do what you wanted. Your reputation had to remain intact. I expected you to marry well." I was astonished by his reply and understood why they had been opposed to my marrying an American. At that time marrying an American was not "marrying well."

My last year at La Fontaine was the hardest. I was preparing for my baccalaureate and had to work very hard, just like all my classmates. No more parties, no more going out with friends (not that it was a great change for me, but all my friends stayed home to study, so I did not feel left out). This was the only time in my life that I lost weight. Food meant less to me than my success on the exam. The day I found out that I had passed, I told my grandmother that I wasn't coming home for dinner. My best friend, Claudine, and I went to a brasserie and I ordered a *chou-*

croute garnie, my favorite. We ate, drank beer, and went to hear Juliette Greco, the French avant-garde singer, perform in a *cave,* a dark cellar music club on the Left Bank. I hadn't been this happy in years.

The next morning, I woke up with a new faith in the possibilities life had to offer me. I was going to fight for what I wanted. I would live alone, travel, attend university. And I'd explore the sensual side of life—pleasures that I had enjoyed in Cairo would come to me in a different way here in Paris. I was no longer "l'Egyptienne"; I was "la Parisienne," with an attitude!

5

My Stepfather

M*y mother had returned* to Paris as the revolution was about to explode. Most European Jews living in Cairo fled to Europe. My mother's best friend, Elie, and her daughter went to Brussels. My mother might have followed them there but feared becoming too dependent on them. And then there were her own family's reprisals if she didn't return to Paris. After all, my aunts whispered behind her back, "*Ses enfants sont là-bas, et il est temps qu'elle soit près d'eux!*" (Her children are there, and it's about time that she be near them!) My mother made a compromise between her duties as a mother and her much-cherished freedom and settled alone in a one-bedroom apartment with a kitchenette in the 16th arrondissement of Paris.

It was a far cry from the luxury she was accustomed to in Cairo, but it had been impossible to take whatever was left of her money out of Egypt because of the revolutionary turmoil. She had salvaged some of her possessions upon leaving, and they cluttered the already cramped space. A magnificent Oriental carpet covered the entire living room floor, and other rugs were rolled and stored in a closet. In one corner, prominently displayed, was a silver tray with a silver tea carafe, creamer, and sugar bowl, the same that used to grace the dining room serving board in my grandparents' home and that now hides in one of my closets. I've tried to pass it on to my children when they got married, but I had no takers. From time to time I take it out, polish it, and set it on my kitchen counter, remembering when I was a child living in Cairo and the tea set would be polished and used for my grandmother's poker day.

I rarely saw my mother in my adolescent days in Paris. Occasionally, she would invite my brother and me out to lunch, never to her apartment. During these lunches, she often complained of being alone, of having no friends and no money. Sometimes, just to spite her, I ordered the most expensive dish on the menu, knowing she'd say nothing. On the way back to our grandmother's house, Eddy would scold me. "You are terrible," he'd say, "why did you order that dish?" I didn't know how to tell him that what I really wanted was to live with her, that hurting her was my way of getting back at her for not taking me in. I knew my mother. I knew that deep down, she felt guilty and scared of me . . . scared that I would turn my back on her as her own mother had done to her. When I asked my uncle Clément why she had no money, he shrugged his shoulders.

"She spent it all on her friends. She wouldn't let us take care of her finances. She trusted strangers, not the family." I wanted to tell my mother that I would gladly give her my inheritance if only she would act like a real mother, but I never found the courage.

I was sixteen when I received a disturbing phone call from my mother. "I am married," she announced. Her tone was curt, businesslike. Resentment and curiosity twisted my voice to shrillness as I fired questions at her. She refused to answer them, instead inviting me to lunch to meet him. "It's an excellent restaurant," my mother said dryly. "We'll have a great meal. The chef is Mira's friend." Her new husband's name made me snicker. And since when did my mother enjoy good food, I wondered. She was always complaining that she was fat and on a diet.

Faugeron was on the Left Bank and had a Michelin star. The day of our lunch, I dressed carefully, thinking I should impress my new stepfather. The word "stepfather" sounded strange. I had not had a father since I was six. What would this one be like? What role would he take in my life? As I pulled on creamy silk stockings and smoothed down my tight navy skirt, I day-dreamed of living in a big house with them. I was hopeful that maybe they would decide they needed a child in their life even if that child was a teenager.

I arrived on time and was greeted by a solemn maître d'hôtel.

As I waited twenty minutes for the newlyweds to show up, I surveyed the restaurant's interior: red velvet banquettes against the wall, tables with white tablecloths and comfortable chairs, landscapes of the Côte d'Or, well-fed and contented diners. My mother made her entrance followed by a man who was holding the door for her and looking at her with adoration. I had to remember to close my mouth, which had opened in shock. Almire Ducreux (a name that might have been given to the protagonist in a seventeenth-century comedy of errors, I thought) was shorter than my mother, with a stiff gray crew cut, a small, expertly trimmed mustache, and a round belly. He was neither handsome nor elegant, and I was totally baffled. Their lateness, it seems, was my mother's fault—she had been fussing with her hair and dress. He apologized to me with a smile as he looked tenderly at my mother. I suddenly realized that he was looking at her as one looks at a lovable child. I liked him already . . . he knew what my mother truly was!

The large menu offered dishes I had never heard of: baked truffle over ashes, partridge terrine, foie gras sautéed in a port sauce, beef *en daube,* stewed hare. I was relieved when Mira asked if I minded his ordering for us. My mother said that she'd have an appetizer and a salad . . . that she really wasn't hungry. This self-abnegating request was repeated countless times in the years to come, while Mira and I plunged with gusto into exquisitely prepared dishes, which made my distant mother even more glum.

My first course arrived engulfed by the most extraordinary,

intoxicating aroma. A lone globe of aluminum foil sat on a white china plate, accompanied by thin slices of buttered toast. I didn't move and simply allowed the scent to waft toward my nose. My stepfather, smiling gently, suggested that I open the foil. I followed every movement he made with his own silver packet. Now a black ball revealed itself, engulfed in steam, its rough, patterned skin reminding me of epidermis under the microscope of my science class. "Slice it thinly and taste it," Mira said with a mock serious tone that belied his amusement. I slid the slice of truffle into my mouth, and I tasted something more sublime than any other food I had ever had. "It's . . . it's . . ." I couldn't begin to describe the joy I felt eating that truffle, an epiphany of the senses, a thrill caressing my adolescent tongue. I grinned at the two of them. My stepfather seemed a little surprised and very pleased by my enthusiasm and my obvious pleasure in eating that truffle. He wondered if I would like to know where they came from and how they were gathered. "Oh, yes!" I exclaimed. But to my great disappointment, my mother, forgotten in our exchange, said dourly, no, next time, when I came to their house. She added that they were moving to a hotel near the Seine until they bought a house. My curiosity about this man who was so unlike my mother was intensified, but I knew better than to ply him with questions. As the next dish arrived, I swore to myself that I would get to know him. If he liked this type of food, I was willing, in my naïve yet pretentious way, to ignore everything else that I felt was strange about him. The next dish was quenelles of *brochet* (pike), a specialty of the north where Mira was born. The quenelles were bathed in two sauces, one white and one pink. As I took a bite, I had a second revelation. This was not any ordinary fish preparation. The airy quenelle dissolved into nothing, leaving my mouth with a creamy, buttery sensation hinting of the sea. Mira explained that the pink sauce was made with tiny fresh shrimps. Seeing that I was enchanted, my stepfather relaxed and began to talk about himself while I savored each mouthful, barely listening.

Almire Ducreux was born in Normandy in 1905, in a small village near Honfleur. His grandfather had been an apple farmer and a maker of Calvados, the apple brandy that Normandy is so famous for. When I met him, he still owned the apple farm but the commercial production of Calvados had been abandoned. Calvados was made only for members of the family and friends. Later, after I had married and moved to New York, Mira would send me 100-proof Calvados in an old bottle of cologne (it was illegal then to ship alcohol by mail). Whenever we received it, we invited friends over to try this powerful drink. We dunked sugar cubes into the golden liquid and sucked on them. The only person I knew who could actually drink the Calvados neat was my friend Adam Santoki, a Lithuanian immigrant, who could swallow it in one gulp and ask for more. I made crêpes with the Calvados and used it to flavor some of my pâtés. I never told Mira that we couldn't drink it, that it was much too strong for us.

When Mira passed his *certificat d'études*, a diploma awarded after completing sixth grade, his teacher told Mira's father that his son was exceptionally bright and should continue to study. Farmers' children usually went to work for their parents at that point and to allow Mira to continue meant that he would have to be sent to the next town to attend a lycée. But in 1916, most men were at war and Mira's father needed him on the farm. Mira begged his father to say yes. "It was my mother," he told me years later. "She knew that by sending me to a lycée, I would be able to get out of the village and become somebody." His father relented and Mira was sent to Deauville. He lived with a family friend of his father, a wine merchant to whom the elder Ducreux sold his production of Calvados. He supported himself while studying by working in restaurants, first as a dishwasher on weekends and nights, then as a vegetable prep. With eyes and ears open, and through his friendships with the young chefs in the kitchen, he learned about restaurant management, purchasing, and cooking techniques. In 1923, when Mira passed his baccalaureate with flying colors, his teachers again appealed to his father, suggesting that Mira study at the university to become a teacher. The elder Ducreux, finally coming to terms with the fact that Mira would never be a farmer, relented. After four years at the university, Mira became the first person in his family to be educated and have a white collar job. Although he was assigned to a school in Deauville, Mira found himself still drawn to the restaurant world. He augmented his meager teaching salary by managing the account books for his chef friends. On crowded weekend nights, he doubled as a maître d'. One night, a regular patron of one of the restaurants, with whom he often had conversations after-hours, asked him to join him for a drink in a private room near the kitchen. This meeting changed Mira's life forever. The patron, a Rothschild, proposed hiring Mira as a manager of a group of hotels he had bought in the Mont d'Or, a watering place in central France. Later, the magnate explained, there would be other partnerships whenever a good business venture came along. Mira jumped at the offer. By the time he met my mother, my stepfather owned several hotels in Paris and two in the Mont d'Or. Yet, in some ways, he remained a farmer's son, a fact that got in the way of a true union with my mother, who was afraid of the disapproving judgments of her own family.

My mother took over the conversation as we finished our quenelles, chatting mindlessly about buying a house, having a garden, going to Mont d'Or to take the baths. I looked over at my stepfather, who was again gazing at her almost stupidly. I knew then that I would not have a place in their lives. My mother would see to that. She did not want her daughter around looking in on her life with a critical stare. As the menu for dessert was handed to me, both of them turned to me. "Colette does not like sweets," said my mother in a nasty tone of voice. "No, Maman," I retorted rudely. "I think I will try the chocolate ganache." Why had I said that? I hated chocolate. My stepfather looked at me, smiled, and said gently, "I don't think chocolate after this meal is a good idea. How about a crêpe filled with *fraises des bois* (tiny wild strawberries)?" Did I like crêpes? I wasn't sure. The only ones were those Georgette used to make, swimming in an orange sauce that made me sick. But it was better than chocolate, and I decided then and there that I liked this man. He was kind, warm, and seemed to understand my mother and our tense relationship. The crêpe came, golden and

Crêpes Stuffed with Fraises des Bois

In the bowl of a food processor place ¾ cup flour with 2 tablespoons sugar, 2 eggs, ⅔ cup beer, ⅓ cup water, 2 tablespoons melted butter, and ½ teaspoon grated lemon rind. Process until all the ingredients are well mixed. Pour the batter into a bowl, cover, and allow it to rest for at least 6 hours. Heat a 5-inch crêpe pan. Butter the pan, add a small quantity of batter, tip the skillet, and let the batter spread over the bottom. If you have poured too much batter, tip the skillet and pour out the excess. Cook the crêpe until the edges are golden brown, flip the crêpe, and cook the other side. Wash and drain 1 pint fraises des bois. Toss them with confectioners' sugar and a few drops of lemon juice. Spread some strawberries in the middle of the crêpe and roll the crêpe around the strawberries. Pour some melted butter over the crêpe, sprinkle with confectioners' sugar, and serve. Makes about 14 crêpes.

lacy. As I took a bite, the soft warm crêpe melted in my mouth and I was left with the slightly tart, perfumed taste of the *fraises des bois*. I must have looked very pleased because my stepfather started to laugh—an honest, hearty laugh that came rolling from the center of his being. I looked up at him and laughed also. We understood one another. My mother, flustered, wanted to know why we were laughing. How could I explain to her my relief in meeting her new husband, and the anxieties I had experienced before going to this lunch—that I would dislike the man, that he would take my mother even farther away from me, that he would reject me as a stepdaughter. All these worries had vanished at my first bite of the crêpe. My stepfather had understood my fears, and had unveiled my profound love of food, which tied him to me.

I did not see my mother for a few weeks after that lunch. My brother did not ask anything about our stepfather, nor did I volunteer information. I needed to keep this relationship to myself for now. Grandmaman Rose ignored their wedding and refused to acknowledge that my mother had remarried. "*C'est un paysan* (He's a peasant)," she said with disdain. "*C'est tout à fait Marceline d'epouser un tel homme* (It's just like Marceline to marry such a man)!" I tried to defend my mother and explain why I liked her new husband but what came out was what a great meal I had! My father's family had a wait-and-see attitude. It took my uncles about three months to accept her husband. I always wondered why they did. Maybe because he was rich, and money was important to them. I never found out but from then on they were nicer to my mother.

One morning my mother called and asked if that Sunday I would come to the hotel in the late afternoon and then go out to dinner. Remembering my previous lunch, I eagerly accepted. The hotel was near the Seine, in the 12th arrondissement, near the Porte de Bercy, quite far from the city's center. It looked second-rate, just a bit shabby, and I was disappointed. As I entered the lobby, a couple was heading for the front desk in front of me. The woman stood slightly behind the man as if to hide. My stepfather, standing behind the reception desk, handed the man a card so he could register. The man seemed to hesitate but then filled out the card and my stepfather handed him the key. "Second floor to the right," he said. "For just two hours, mind you." I was fascinated by the whole exchange. My stepfather was running a love hotel by the hour! Did my mother know it? She was often so naïve. And how would my brother, prudish and stuck-up, react to that news? I stood frozen in embarrassment. Mira had not seen me. Should I go out and come back in or just ignore the whole incident and call out his name? I decided that I really didn't care what the hotel was used for. I giggled and thought of my great-aunt in Cairo, my grand-mother's sister, who had run a genteel whorehouse for widowers and whom the family, except for my grandmother, had cut off. I remembered suddenly the jovial atmosphere of the place and my great-aunt feeding me nuts while she and my grandmother talked. I had loved going there as a child. The men played cards

with intense good humor while the young women fussed over
me.

Mira greeted me warmly and led me to the apartment behind
the desk. My mother was sitting in an armchair in a large, ugly
room knitting near the window. She seemed stuck to the chair,
too complacent and heavy. "Colette, look at what I am knitting . . . Mira's daughter is expecting her fourth child." I had forgotten that Mira had another family. My mother seemed very
interested in her future stepgrandchild. I felt jealous and angry
and sat pouting in a corner. She'd never knitted for me. Mira
also had a son, who was engaged to be married. "Mira doesn't
like his fiancée," my mother confided to me, with obvious pleasure at having something to gossip about. "He is a lawyer and
she is . . . well . . . vulgar," as if being a lawyer made him more
elegant. I wanted to ask my mother about the hotel but was too
shy. Was I supposed to know that couples could meet and make
love in two hours? Or that you could pay a woman for these two
hours? I decided that, as usual, it was better not to ask my
mother about things she disliked.

The dinner in the local restaurant was nothing like our first
lunch. It was a small bistro, and for the first time I had *hareng
saur*, delicate herring filets in oil and onions served with warm
potatoes. This dish was followed by an *omelette aux fines herbes*
and an apple tart. It was all tasty but didn't come close to the
intense experience I had at our first lunch. During dinner I
learned that Mira was revamping his hotels in the Mont d'Or
and would start out in a month, going every weekend to search

for two-star chefs to run the restaurants in the summer. Mira asked me if I'd like to join them. I hesitated, but the promise of fine cuisine was tempting. I could always decline later on if I didn't enjoy myself. Most important, it was a way to ingratiate myself. On the spur of the moment, I agreed.

For the next month, I did not see my mother. I learned that they had bought a house in the suburbs, in Maison-Lafitte, about forty minutes from the Etoile. "I have a garden," my mother said proudly over the phone, "and nice neighbors." My mother with a garden! She had never planted a single flower, nor could she cook. But I was jealous that now she not only had a husband but also a house, a garden, and all of this without a thought for me. I felt nostalgic for my Egyptian grandparents' house, the noise of the women chatting on the terrace, and Ahmet! Ahmet, our cook, was my best friend when I lived in Cairo. Oh God, how I wanted to be plopped again on his kitchen counter, looking at him cooking *ful medamas,* the tiny brown fava beans, braised and seasoned. I wanted to sink my teeth into a hot sandwich of *ful* redolent of cumin and lemon. . . . It seemed like a fading dream.

Our first weekend search took place in February. We drove to Fleurines, about fifty-six kilometers from Paris, where, Mira explained, a young chef was making a name for himself. During the ride, which lasted three hours, I never spoke, feeling that I had made a mistake in being there. I had to forget about creating a relationship with my mother's husband, as it would lead nowhere and just hurt me. This was going to be the last time I spent a weekend with them. When we reached Fleurines, Mira had trouble locating the restaurant. It was tucked away in a backstreet. When we finally found it, we were charmed by the intimate dining room, with its lace curtains, empty bottles of wine serving as candleholders, and a small bar in a corner where two men were smoking and drinking wine. As soon as we sat down, my mother whined that she wasn't hungry and would have just a tidbit. Mira turned to me with an air of complicity and said, "I'm famished. You?" "Me, too," I assured him. So we began a feast. The meal started with a delicate mousse of foie gras served with onion preserves. Mira watched me as I took a bite. "How do you think it was made?" he asked me. I had no idea. "Close your eyes. Imagine the spices. Do you think there is wine in the mousse? What makes the onion jam so tangy?" I tried and failed. Red wine? No. But certainly cream? Yes. The spices? I couldn't guess. Lemon juice? No. I gave up and continued to eat, feeling flushed and excited by what seemed to me a guessing game of the senses.

The next dish was fish baked with caramelized endives. Again my stepfather asked questions about how the fish was prepared. "You see, Colette," he said somewhat gravely, "to appreciate a dish you must know what's in it. It is important to remember the taste. Food is memory. If you can remember this lunch in a week, then the food was memorable and worth your while. I will teach you."

Mousse de Foie avec Compote d'Onions
(Liver Mousse with Onion Jam)

Trim 1 pound fresh chicken livers, removing any gristle. In a large skillet melt 2 tablespoons butter. When the butter is hot add the chicken livers and sauté for 3 minutes. Sprinkle the livers with 2 tablespoons dried tarragon, salt, and pepper, and pour 2 tablespoons cognac over them. Ignite. When the flame dies down cook the livers for another 2 minutes. Remove from the heat. Place the chicken livers with the butter in a food processor. Add 1 cup heavy cream and process until all the livers are puréed. Strain the liver mixture through a fine sieve. Correct the seasoning with freshly ground pepper and ½ teaspoon nutmeg. Pour the mousse into a 1-quart mold or 4 small molds. Place the mold in a baking pan. Add 4 cups water to the pan. Bake in a preheated 325-degree oven for 20 minutes. Remove from the oven and cool. In a bowl mix 2 envelopes unflavored gelatin. Add 3 tablespoons water and mix well. Add 2 cups chicken bouillon. Pour the mixture into a small saucepan and cook for 3 minutes, or until all the gelatin has melted. Cool, then slowly pour the gelatin on top of the mousse and refrigerate. Serve the mousse with onion jam. Serves 6 to 8.

Onion Jam

*Peel 1 pound small onions and place them
on a rack in the oven above a pan of boiling
water. Bake the onions in a preheated 325-
degree oven for 20 minutes until nearly tender.
Remove the onions to a platter and dry with
paper towels. In a large skillet melt ½ cup butter; when the butter is hot add the onions, 2
tablespoons brown sugar, 1 tablespoon chopped
fresh rosemary, and salt and pepper. Mix well
so that all the onions are well coated with the
sugar. Lower the heat, cover, and simmer for 30
minutes, stirring from time to time. If the
onions seem too dry, add more butter. Remove
the onion jam from the heat and cool. Spoon the
jam into glass jars and refrigerate until ready
to use.*

For the next three months, I followed my stepfather in his
quest for new chefs. Both of us ignored my mother, who always
repeated the same litany: "I'm not very hungry . . . I'll have
something light." Meanwhile, she was growing mysteriously
plump. During the lunch or dinner, my stepfather and I played
our guessing game, trying to unravel the intricacies of our meal's
preparation. When the chef came out at the end of the meal to
meet Mira, we'd ask him what herbs and spices he used, how
the soufflé was composed, whether the meat was marinated
overnight. In three months I had acquired a sophisticated

vocabulary of ingredients, spices, methods of cooking. If I guessed correctly, my stepfather would grant me ten points. A hundred points were worth a present. This was how I went ski-

Artichoke à la Barigoule

This is an old recipe from Provence. In the sixteenth century, "Barigoule" referred to a type of mushroom with which the artichokes were cooked. The Barigoule mushroom disappeared from Provence but the name of the dish has remained. Prepare 16 very small spring artichokes. Cut off about 1½ inches of leaves from the top. You should have only about 3 inches from the stem. With a teaspoon remove the center choke of each artichoke. Cut off the stems and remove the tough leaves from the bottoms. Rub each artichoke with lemon to prevent it from turning brown. Peel ½ pound onions and 4 shallots and scrape and wash 2 carrots. Place all the vegetables in a food processor. Process until all the ingredients are minced. In an ovenproof saucepan heat 2 tablespoons olive oil. Spread the vegetables on the bottom of the saucepan. Sprinkle the artichokes with salt and pepper inside and out and place them on top of the vegetables. Add 2 more tablespoons olive oil, 1 cup white wine, and 1 cup water. Add 3 sprigs of fresh thyme. Cover and bake in a preheated 325-degree oven for 2 hours. Serve hot or cold as an appetizer. Serves 4.

ing at Christmas, got a new dress at Easter, a silk scarf in my favorite color. Mira and I became great friends. We did not talk much during these trips; we just ate, and the food was our bond that grew stronger and stronger every year.

As my relationship with my stepfather solidified, other problems arose. Mira had decided that Claude, his son, should marry me. For weeks Mira talked to me about Claude, his future as a judge, and how we'd have a great life together. I was turning seventeen, had just passed my baccalaureate, and was thinking of taking the exam to enter the Pasteur Institute. Claude and I had met several times at family functions, barely talking to one another. He was short like his father, with thinning auburn hair and a receding hairline. I called him *"le hareng saur,"* from a poem I loved by Jacques Prevert, in which a man with fish eyes is described. His thin lips rarely smiled and he lacked joie de vivre and an appreciation of fine cuisine, both of which were important attributes for me in a future husband (I knew that already at seventeen!). I disliked his pedantic conversation and his dry humor. His fiancée was always there, shunned by my mother and Mira.

One day Claude phoned and asked me to dinner at a café on the Champs Elysées. As we sat down to dinner, sipping a glass of red wine, Claude announced that in two months he would marry Suzanne. "I don't want to marry you," he said. "I don't either," I replied. "I don't even like you." Claude's nostrils flared when he heard my nasty retort. But he needed my help, so his expression softened. He pleaded with me to convince my stepfather that under no circumstances would I marry his son. I promised that I would try and we finished our dinner in silence, having nothing much in common.

The next weekend, Mira told me that we were going to go to Salon-de-Provence in the south of France to look at a new inn and talk to the chef. The inn, housed in a former convent, the Abbeye de Saint Croix, was perched on top of a hill and had a magnificent view of the valley below. As we were waiting for dinner that evening, I asked Mira to take a walk through the herb garden that the chef had enthusiastically talked about. As we walked together, I told Mira I could not marry his son. I hoped he would understand and still consider me his daughter. Mira sighed, picked a sprig of lavender, and handed it to me.

Years later, when Jimmy, my American fiancé, came for me in Paris, the only one who greeted him with open arms was my stepfather. They would sit together in the garden and talk about French politics, chain-smoking. When we caused a scandal by living together in Munich before we were even married, Mira was the only one who stood by my side and defended me. When I announced that I was going to marry this American, my brother sent me a letter saying, "In our family one doesn't marry Americans! They are uncultured and barbaric." I never forgave him.

Mira died in 1961, weeks before coming to the United States to visit me and my new family. My mother, widowed for the second time and alone in Paris, moved to New York, right across the street from our house, more than ever a stranger to me.

6

The Boyfriends

I *was sixteen and didn't have a boyfriend.* Claudine and Nicole didn't have one either. I was baffled. Claudine, after all, was pretty—curly golden hair, voluptuous body, even features—and Nicole, sharp-featured and skinny, was extremely charming and worldlier than I. Her brother was an agent for famous movie stars, and she'd tell us about parties he gave for his clients where she met highly ambitious teens who wanted to break into show business. When I look now at pictures of us at that age, I realize that we were actually frumpy, badly dressed, and not à la mode. I never read fashion magazines; worse, I neglected the newspapers and had little awareness of what was happening in the world around me. Like every Parisian youth, I loved popular singers like Charles Trenet, Georges Brassens, and Juliette Greco. I read Prevert's poetry and could recite his poem *Liberté* with tears in my eyes. I read romantic novels and dreamed of meeting a young man who would rescue me from my abusive grandmother. But that winter nothing happened. Boys from the nearby school that my brother attended sometimes came and stood on the other side of the street ogling the girls as they filed out of the front gate. They whistled, and sometimes a girl crossed over to talk to them. My friend Judith knew one of the boys, Charles, a tall seventeen-year-old with a very short haircut just like the American actors he had seen in the movies. He was in the grade above us, and Judith reported that he was very sophisticated, had read André Gide, and could explain Gide's philosophy to her, although it went right over her head. She joined him after school and they walked together to the métro. Sometimes he even rode with her until she reached home. She whispered to us how much she liked him, but she couldn't go out with him officially, nor could he come to her house. Her family insisted that she receive only Jewish suitors. I often wondered what I would do if I had a boyfriend. Would my grandmother let me go out with him if he was not Jewish? I knew my brother had a girlfriend; I had caught him calling her from home but I never mentioned anything to my grandmother. We both knew not to involve her, and after that day my brother was nicer to me. Despite our fondness for each other, Claudine and I never talked about our problems, so I never knew if she was upset by our lack of boyfriends. We never talked about sex either. I had not left the convent in Cairo long enough to forget what the nuns used to say to us nearly every day: "Don't flirt with boys; stay pure until you are engaged and know that you are getting married. Virginity is the most precious gift of all." *Precious gift? For whom?* At night, when I was aching with loneliness or felt the need to be hugged or kissed as in the novels I read, I ended up in the kitchen, barefoot in my nightgown, eating thick slices of *saucisson sec* with a piece of baguette. If I had been older I would have drowned the salami with a glass of wine, but as in every French household, you drank wine only at meals. Instead, I washed my midnight snack down with buttermilk. Once in a while my grandmother caught me and berated me with her shrill voice. "You are going to get fat! You should not eat again late at night. Go to bed!" She never invited me to chat with her.

Before leaving the convent to come to France, I had sometimes heard the older girls in the dormitory talk about masturbation. I did not quite know what they meant, but I had heard them discussing caressing themselves at night. I was afraid to ask or even to talk about it. *What if it was a sin? What would happen to me? And what about my virginity? Would I lose it?* I tried once to ask one of the older girls but she blushed and answered that I was too young. None of us, I was sure, dared ask the nuns, and now, in Paris, I had no one to talk to.

One day, Paulette, a flighty girl with whom we were acquainted, announced that over the weekend she had met a young man, and that she had gone dancing with him with her parents' permission. He kissed her on the lips and did much more. *Much more?* We all wanted to know, but proud as a peacock, Paulette moved away and left us in the dark, our imaginations on fire. *What had happened? Did she go to bed with him?* We looked at her for signs, but she seemed no different than she had the week before. For the next few days, I tried to catch her alone to ask her questions, but she would just smile and walk away. I was frustrated. I looked through the bookshelves in my grandfather's library, read and reread Colette's stories, but found nothing that would help.

In March we all had to have a physical checkup. A doctor was to come to the school and perfunctorily check our heartbeat, blood pressure, and teeth. If he felt anything was amiss, a note would be sent to our parents and then we had to be thoroughly examined by our own doctor. I hated my gym class, held Thursday afternoons, and instead wanted to walk on the Left Bank and explore Paris. Claudine had special dispensation and could miss gym; I yearned to go home with her too. I told Judith, Claudine, and Nicole how miserable I was about having to go to gym class. Judith had a brilliant idea. "When the doctor comes and it is your turn, don't take the elevator. Run up the stairs very fast and chew on blotting paper. It will raise your body temperature and the doctor will think you have heart disease." It worked! My grandmother got a letter from the school stating that I might have something wrong with my heart, and until I was checked out by my own physician I could not take gym class. I was elated. For the next two weeks, until my grandmother made an appointment with our doctor, I was free to be with Claudine and roam the streets of Paris.

Our doctor was a man in his late thirties, and as we sat down in his office, my grandmother explained that I had lived in Egypt, that I had been in Paris only one year, and that the school doctor who had examined me thought I had something wrong with my heart. The doctor stared at me and I stared back, mentally imploring him to find something wrong with me. He then took me to his examining room and listened carefully to my heart while my grandmother looked on. Again I stared directly at the doctor, right into his eyes. I remembered my Egyptian grandmother saying that all Palacci women were witches and if I wanted something badly enough I could send a message with my eyes. The doctor cocked his head in confusion, turned to my grandmother, and said in a low voice, *"Elle a des yeux de boudoir; ils sont superbes mais elle a aussi un soufle au coeur, donc pas de gymnastique!"* ("She has bedroom eyes. They are superb, but she also has a heart murmur, so no gym classes!") I felt elated but then he added that I had to be on a diet and not eat any fat. What about butter, cream, cheese, and all the things I loved? "On a diet," he repeated, "for at least two months." For years after that I never knew if I had a *soufle au coeur,* and I don't know if he felt he had given me what I wanted, but I had to pay the price. Once outside, my grandmother said in an angry voice, "You are impossible! What did you do to him? Did you say or make a sign for him to say such a thing about your eyes?" I denied doing anything but thought of my Egyptian grandmother. Yes, she was right; maybe, after all, I was a witch! I often told my own children that I was a witch and that I could foresee the future in a coffee cup. I would read the dregs of a cup of Turkish coffee and tell them what I thought would happen to them or answer their questions by reading their fates in the cards. Sometimes I was right. It seems my daughter Marianne has inherited my witchcraft . . . or at least my talent for guessing correctly; she has confessed to reading Turkish coffee grounds for her friends.

Back home that night, as I undressed I stood naked in front of the mirror. I looked at my body. My breasts were large but firm and I had a very small waist and round hips. I thought I looked like the picture of my grandmother when she was young. I was born in the wrong century, one hundred years too late. Perhaps if I had been born in the nineteenth century, I would have been considered a beauty. I looked at my eyes again and saw nothing. What did he mean by *des yeux de boudoir?* I slowly caressed my breasts and thought *if only there was some man who would do this to me.* I felt warmth all over my body and, closing my eyes, I imagined him kissing me. Suddenly I was brought back to earth by a knock on the door. My brother was saying that my grandmother was not feeling well and would I make her something hot to drink? Quickly I put on a dressing gown and went into the kitchen to make her some hot tea. Once she had sipped her tea and gone to sleep, I went into my room and tried to recapture the feeling I had had while looking at myself in the mirror. The magic had gone and I was simply hungry. My grandmother had made me eat salad and cold ham that evening, while she and my brother regaled themselves on soft scrambled eggs with heavy cream and truffle juice served with boiled new potatoes, a dish I loved. As I opened the *garde-manger*, I found the remains of stuffed artichokes that had been served the night before. The stuffing was delicious: a mixture of chopped mushrooms and black olives in a light vinaigrette. They were as good cold as they were hot and I devoured two of them. I felt better. The next day, with a note from the doctor and one from my grandmother, I was excused from gym for the remaining months of school.

One day in early May my brother came to me and asked if I would like to join his friends and him in a play they were going to produce for their school. The play, Gide's *Oedipus Rex,* was going to be performed in the local theater. They need a woman to play the role of Oedipus' mother and they had found no one. I was astonished. *My brother asking me to join him?* I eagerly accepted and was told that the following Saturday I would go with him to rehearsal. Meanwhile could I start learning my lines?

That Saturday I went with my brother to his school to meet the cast. There were many boys standing around. My brother explained that they were the chorus and then took me to meet the three other important characters of the play. Gérard, a boy of about eighteen, was Oedipus. He was shorter than my brother, with intense brown eyes and a mop of unruly brown hair. He was wearing baggy corduroy pants and a black turtleneck sweater. "Hi, what's your name? You're Eddy's girlfriend?" "Of course not!" I countered, indignant. "I am his sister, and my name is Colette." Suddenly, all the other boys standing next to Gérard burst out laughing. "We saw him with you so often that we thought you were his girl. He never told us he had a sister." I blushed, angry with my brother for not telling them in advance that I was his sister. *Was he ashamed of me?* As I was about to turn toward him, a tall blond boy with deep blue eyes came forward and, extending his hand, said kindly, "My name is Georges. Welcome aboard. I play Creon, Oedipus' uncle and your brother. I am very happy that you agreed to be one of us."

All week long I waited for Saturday and the rehearsal. My brother was the director and in charge of the production. I soon realized that I was not a very good actress and I worried a lot that they would be tired of telling me all the time to be "natural." I tried hard and learned my lines expertly, but what excited me the most was what took place after the rehearsals. Georges, Gérard, my brother, and I would end up in a café. The three of them discussed politics, theater, books, and sometimes girls. Neither Georges nor Gérard seemed to have a girlfriend, or at least I never saw them with girls. As I listened, I made mental notes of the books and authors they talked about and bought them that same day. I became a voracious reader. I didn't always understand what I read but I tried to keep up with the three of them. Politics became my favorite subject. Gérard leaned to the left, Georges to the center, and my brother was the conservative one. They argued about General MacArthur, the atomic bomb, the validity of a war in Korea. I listened carefully. A year later, when I was in the twelfth grade and General MacArthur threatened to drop an atomic bomb on Korea, I, along with all my school friends, marched on the American Embassy in protest. It was the first time that I involved myself in a political demonstration and I felt very proud. Later there would be other marches, but this one was the direct result of sitting in a café for hours, listening to three young men arguing politics, two of whom I had fallen in love with.

We'd all go out to dine in cheap bistros. I always tried not to eat too much in front of these wonderful boys, realizing quickly that food and wine were not important to them. They ate and drank without tasting what they were eating or drinking. I usually chose the same thing: *frites* and a *sandwich au jambon.* Sometimes I took a *plat du jour,* especially if it was a *blanquette de veau,* a veal stew with lemon and cream. I loved that dish, and even today I make it whenever I feel nostalgic. The rehearsals took three months of blissful Saturdays. Even after three months I wasn't better than in the first few days of rehearsals. The day of the performance, my jitters were overshadowed by a feeling of doom. *What would I do on Saturdays? Would I see them again?* I wanted to perform well that night; maybe if they produced another play, they would ask me again. I was dressed in a long, narrow black dress, my hair done up in long curls falling over my forehead and tied in the back with golden cords. For the first time in my life I had makeup on; Georges's mother had painted me with lipstick, rouge, and dark mascara on my eyelashes. I looked at myself in the mirror of the ladies' room. My eyes were copper-colored edged in green, and the dress and high heels made me look ten years older. As I left the ladies' room, Georges and Gérard, who were standing outside, looked at me and together said, *"merde!"* I must have blushed because they both became quite embarrassed and left me without another word. *What was wrong? Was I not beautiful? I am sure, I* thought, *it is the makeup.* I wanted to cry. I followed them back-stage, hoping still that they would say something about how I looked. But they were busy rehearsing their lines and I did the same.

Blanquette de Veau

Ask the butcher to cut a breast of veal into 1½-inch pieces—about 3 pounds. In a sauce-pan heat 1 tablespoon olive oil with 1 table-spoon butter. Add the veal and brown on all sides. Add 1 onion, stuck with 1 clove and 1 bay leaf and sprinkle the veal with 1 tablespoon sage. Cover with 2½ cups chicken bouillon. Bring to a boil, lower the heat, and simmer, covered, for 1 hour. Add salt and pepper to taste, 2 carrots, scraped and thinly sliced, and ½ pound mushrooms, quartered. Cook for another 15 minutes, or until the carrots are done. In a bowl beat 2 egg yolks with ½ cup heavy cream and the juice of 1 lemon. While stirring, add 2 tablespoons of the hot broth from the veal. Pour the egg/lemon mixture into the veal stew. Keep it hot but do not cook or boil. Serve the veal with the sauce and steamed couscous or boiled potatoes. Serves 4 to 6.

The theater was filled with students, parents, and teachers. My grandmother had told me that she wasn't coming because she had accepted a dinner invitation for that night. I was hurt and at the same time relieved, since I'd be able to attend the cast party after the play. My brother was in the wings, nervously pacing. This was his production, and the way he looked at me, I knew I had to be good. Toward the end of the play, when Jocasta, Oedipus' mother and wife, realizes what has happened to her and her family, I, too, realized that this was the end for me. There would be no more Saturdays to rehearse, no more discussions in the café; life would be as it had been before the play. I must have expressed my sorrow as I recited the lines. As the curtain fell down, the audience roared with delight, and Georges and Gérard hugged me; even my brother smiled at me. I had not disappointed them. At the cast party, Georges, Gérard, and my brother were surrounded while I was ignored or thought I was. I left early without saying goodbye to anyone. That night in bed, I cried myself to sleep. *How or when would I see both boys again?* I was just Eddy's sister and for them, I was the girl who had solved their problem. I had played the role of the queen, had played it well, and that was that.

The next day in school, my friends gathered around me, plying me with questions. *What was it like? Did people like the play? Did I meet anyone interesting at the party? What was going to happen next? Was I going to be an actress?* I exaggerated somewhat about my success. No, I did not want to be an actress. I wanted to be a scientist. No, there was no boyfriend waiting for me, I told them with bitterness. Disappointed by my answers, my companions dropped the subject and we all went to the café next door where I ordered two croissants and a large café au lait to drown my sorrow.

That Saturday, Claudine and I walked down the Boulevard Saint-Germain, stopping at the church. While Claudine was dutifully admiring the architecture, I lit a candle to the Virgin Mary, praying that Georges and Gérard would call or at least would want to put on another play. "Why are you lighting a candle?" asked Claudine suspiciously, standing behind me. I had to think quickly. By now Claudine knew that my family was Jewish but I never talked about myself being Catholic. "Superstition," I said as I pushed her to the door. This was not the time to tell her my story.

We continued our walk along the boulevard, admiring the new boutiques and entering the bookstores where, like everyone else, we flipped through the new books, reading a page or two. Saint-Germain was then the center of the avant-garde, and the streets were packed with students, foreigners, and politicians. We walked to Café Flore where Sartre and Simone de Beauvoir sat for hours arguing. The café was packed with girls dressed in black, drinking strong coffee, while the boys in turtleneck sweaters smoked acrid Gitanes. I felt dowdy in my navy dress and flat shoes and bare legs. I was so unfashionable! Later, I walked behind the Church of Saint-Germain-des-Prés to the open food and seafood market and passed mounds of oysters, clams, shrimps, small artichokes with their stems still on, and white asparagus, my favorite. I stood there wishing I could buy everything. I imagined myself having a small apartment, shopping for food, and cooking a sumptuous dinner for Georges and Gérard. Just before heading home, I bought some *crevettes grises* (tiny, pale cooked shrimps) that I munched on in the métro.

A week later, as I was leaving school, I saw Gérard and Georges waving to me from across the street to come and join them. My heart beating, my knees trembling, I crossed, wanting to look indifferent but only managing to smile foolishly as I approached them. "Come to the café with us . . . we want to talk to you!" My prayers were answered! They were going to ask me to join them for another play! I felt light as a bird, and as I crossed the street, I reviewed in my mind what I was going to say when both boys asked me to help them. Georges asked me if I wanted to have something to eat. I said no, just coffee, although I was starving and would have liked a *chien-chaud* (a hot dog in a baguette), a recent discovery that I craved every afternoon. There was a moment of silence while we waited for our coffee. I looked at Georges—really looked at him—for the first time. He was tall, thin, with blondish hair, earnest blue eyes, and a long French nose. He wore blue pants, an elegant white shirt, and a navy blue sweater wrapped around his shoulders. My gaze went to Gérard and I smiled inadvertently. As usual Gérard's clothes were in disarray. His brown sweater had holes at the elbows, his curly brown hair was too long, and his eyeglasses gave his face an owlish look. They were broken and held together with tape. He was shorter than Georges but just as thin. I felt comfortable with him and liked his sense of humor. The silence continued, and both of them were looking down at their coffee. After a while I coughed, looked up, and said, "Well, how are you both? I missed the rehearsals . . . it was a good play," and waited. Suddenly Georges started to talk: "Colette . . . this is hard to say . . . but we . . ." and he stopped, blushing deeply. "We are both in love with you. We don't know whom you . . . you . . . like best. We've been fighting and have decided that you have to . . . to . . . choose." I looked at both incredulously. Georges was red as a beet and Gérard was looking down at his shoes. *Choose? But how? Which one? This was ridiculous!* "I don't know . . . I love you both . . . I miss you both. How must I choose?" I stuttered, frightened by their earnestness. *What sort of change would this bring?* "You can kiss each one in turn and then decide," Gérard said with a smile. I looked down at my empty cup of coffee, wondering what the correct answer was. I had never kissed a boy before, nor did I know how. Georges then said in a whisper, "Come! Let's go next door inside the apartment building and kiss." I got up and followed him like a stupid puppy. We entered the courtyard of the building next door, and he embraced me awkwardly and kissed me with a closed, dry-lipped mouth. *He's too tall,* I thought, *and his lips are chapped.* I wanted to tell him to try again but was afraid. We went out on the street again and Gérard was waiting outside the building. Now it was his turn. I suddenly felt like laughing. *If only my grandmother could see me now,* I thought, *she would have a* real *heart attack!* Gérard bent down toward me, tilted my head up with his hand under my chin, and looked into my eyes. "You have such beautiful eyes and I *do* love you." This was unexpected and I felt as if a wave were hitting me in the chest. I wanted to be in his arms; I wanted to be kissed right away. I held on to him, lifted my head toward him, and kissed him. As we went out, I looked at Georges and felt sorry for him. "It's him," I said, pointing to Gérard. "I'm so sorry. I really like you, but I love him." Georges walked away, his head bent, shuffling his feet. Years later, after I had gotten married, I met Georges again in Paris. He was still handsome and so very proper. We laughed together, recalling our foiled kisses in the doorway.

From then on Gérard met me outside the school gate and walked me home. Sometimes we stopped at a café and sat for an hour. I listened while Gérard talked about his dream of becoming a poet. I hid the poems he wrote to me under my mattress. At night I'd take them out and read them again and again, as well as his many letters in which he revealed his carnal desires for me. Very soon I had a bundle of letters under the mattress, and I was afraid that my grandmother would find them.

On Saturdays he took me to listen to black jazz singers who were a hit in Paris. He gave me books to read, records to listen to, and he taught me to read the newspaper every day. "You have to know what is going on in the world, Colette. . . . You have to take a stand and for that you must be informed." It is at that time that I became hooked on politics. We read *Le Monde* "to be in the know," Gérard would say; and *l'Humanité,* a communist rag. "I am not a communist," Gérard would explain, "but you have to defend the poor and the working class." Sometimes he took me out to lunch. "I found a great place for *frites,* you want some?" and we trotted to a special little hole in the wall and devoured a plate of *frites* with salt and *boudin blanc* (white veal sausages). After lunch, we walked hand in hand, and suddenly he would stop in the middle of the street, hug me, and kiss me deeply. I was in heaven.

One day Gérard announced that his parents were going away for the weekend and would I come to his apartment for lunch? I told my grandmother that I was going to Claudine's house to work with her, told Claudine that I wanted to be with Gérard, and that if my grandmother called, we were both out. Gérard lived on the Left Bank in an old apartment house. Both his parents were university professors. The apartment—long, narrow, and dark—was filled with books, old furniture, paintings on the walls, so very different from ours. Gérard's room was small with posters on the wall, books on the floor, and papers scattered all over his desk. "I am writing a novel," Gérard said. "I will let you read a chapter." There was a studio bed in one corner. Gérard hugged me, then kissed me, and pushed me gently toward the bed. I lay down stiffly, not moving, my legs tightly closed together. Gérard started to undo my blouse. I was petrified. In my mind I saw Mère de Rousiers looking at me, and I could hear her voice saying, *Don't, Colette . . . you must not . . . it is a sin.* The image was so strong that I jumped up and said in a trembling voice, "I can't . . . not now . . . I must go home. I love you but . . ." I bolted out of the room, put on my jacket, and ran to the métro. As I sat down, I thought how ridiculous I was, that I was surely going to lose him. I hated myself, my life, everything. When I got home I was relieved to see that my grandmother was out. I ran to the telephone and called Gérard. "I am sorry . . . I was scared . . . please forgive me. Next week I will be there . . . I promise." Gérard calmed me and said not to worry, that he understood. He was going away for ten days but when he returned, he would meet me at school, and meanwhile he would write to me.

Gérard kept his word. A few days later a letter came for me. I had asked the concierge to just hand me my mail and not give it to my grandmother. The letter spoke of kissing me, of stroking my breasts, of making love and how wonderful it would all be. I read and reread the letter before putting it with the others under my mattress. A few days later, when I came home from school, my grandmother called me into her room. As I entered, I saw my letters in her hand. "How dare you! You are like a whore! Having a lover at sixteen! I forbid you to see him again. I will call your uncle Clément and tell him about this! Go to your room." I was crushed. *What was I going to do?* I wanted to call Gérard but I did not know where he was. I wanted to talk to someone but to whom? The next day, as I left the school, I saw my uncle Clément's car. "Get in, I have to talk to you." Once in the car, he spoke about our family's name, reputation, how young I was, that I had time to have a boyfriend, that for now I had to abide by my grandmother's wishes. "I hate her," I said.

"Why do I have to live with her?" "You are too young to live alone; you have to protect your name." I looked at him and said in a nasty voice, "And you, you live with your mistress! You don't protect your name." As soon as I said that, I was sorry. Clément had always been very kind to me. "I am sorry I said that. I was just angry. I will only see him on weekends outside. I won't go to his house, I promise." Clément drove me home and handed me some money. "Buy yourself something nice; you will feel better afterward." I wanted to return the money, but I could not hurt his feelings again. He did not understand what I felt but he meant well. For him, as for all his generation and class, money was always the solution.

A few days later when I tried to call Gérard I was told he was still away. For several weeks afterward, I kept on calling, not understanding what had happened. Where was he? I finally broke down and asked my brother. He told me that my grandmother had called his parents and had asked them to be sure that Gérard never came close to me. I cried and screamed at my grandmother who looked at me with scorn. "You're like your mother; nothing good will ever come your way." I never saw him again. Years later I learned that he became a professor like his parents.

One day in July while we were having lunch, the telephone rang. Eddy went to answer and came back, telling my grandmother, "There is a young man on the phone. He speaks English

and says that he is the son of Anne Rossant. He wants to talk to
you." My grandmother picked up the phone and spoke in
English. She sounded excited. When she came back to the table,
she said, "It was the son of an old friend of ours from America.
He is coming to lunch tomorrow with his friends. Colette, I told
him that you will show him Paris." The next day my grandmother decided to make a quiche Lorraine followed by a tomato
salad and raspberries with crème fraîche for dessert. I was sent
shopping, told to buy cheeses and bread, and to make the
tomato salad. By noon everyone was impatient to see this young
American and his friends. Finally the doorbell rang. I opened
the door and was faced with a very tall young man, with gray-
green eyes, thin, and very handsome. "I am Jimmy. You must be
Colette. This is my friend Les." I shook hands and thought, *My
English is terrible. How do I speak to him?* We sat down to lunch
and Jimmy spoke about his mother, told us his father was dead
and that his brother was working in England. They were on
their way to Italy and Denmark, maybe Greece, but wanted to
visit Paris first. "This food is great. I've never had such a wonderful tomato salad. Who made it?" I said I did and he smiled at
me and said again and again, "Great salad . . . great salad." Now
he jokes that he married me because of the tomato salad. For
the next week we were inseparable. I showed him Paris, took
him and Les to the opera, where we were thrown out because
we laughed so much, visited the Left Bank and every church
and important building that he had heard of. Gérard was forgotten. Again I was in love, this time with a tall American. I followed

Tomato Salad

Place 4 large tomatoes in a bowl, cover with boiling water, and allow the tomatoes to soak for 5 minutes. Drain and refresh under cold running water. In a large salad bowl mix together ½ teaspoon salt, freshly ground black pepper, 1 teaspoon lemon juice, 2 tablespoons olive oil, 1 garlic clove, minced, and 2 shallots, minced. Add 10 fresh tarragon leaves. Mix well. Peel the tomatoes (the skin should easily slide away). Thinly slice the tomatoes, add to the lemony dressing, toss, and serve. Serves 4.

him everywhere, sat by his side while he sketched, admiring his drawings. "I want to be an architect and build cities as great as these," he said to me. "I am going to architectural school when I go back." I did not want him to leave but never said anything to him. The day before he left to continue his trip, he had lunch again at our house. Again I made a tomato salad to serve with my grandmother's *boeuf en gelée* (beef in aspic). Jimmy was sitting in front of me, playing with my foot. I lost my shoe and suddenly I heard my grandmother say, "Colette, remove the plates and bring in the ice cream." I was embarrassed, as I could not find my shoe, which had ended up under Jimmy's chair. I dropped my napkin, bent down, and Jimmy pushed the shoe toward me. We were safe. Just as he was leaving, my grandmother invited him to Hendaye on the Atlantic Coast, where we were going to spend a month. Jimmy thanked her, took the address, but said probably not as he wanted to see Denmark. He kissed me good-bye on the cheek and said that he hoped to see me on his way back. I was sad to see him go and felt alone and miserable. I did not know if he liked me or not but I knew that I loved him.

In the next few weeks we got several postcards from Jimmy addressed to the family. Nothing special for me. He was having a great time, he wrote, and hoped to see us in September. In early August, we left for Hendaye, a small town not too far from Biarritz where my grandparents spent many vacations in their house before the war. Hendaye had a beautiful beach, and the small hotel where we stayed was more like a pension. The food was great, especially the fish and the seafood. My favorite was a bouillabaisse with sardines—a rich fish broth simmered with fennel and served with sardines and toast covered with a spicy aioli. After a long morning swim, I devoured mounds of deep-fried tiny fish or rich *rillettes* spread on country bread served with a green salad. But my favorite dish was mussels cooked with ham and lots of garlic. At night we had fish with a red vinegar sauce or fresh tuna with green olives and roast potatoes. I stuffed myself with strawberries and peaches and somewhat forgot for a while Jimmy and my loneliness.

One day, after we had been in Hendaye for two weeks or so, we received a telegram from Jimmy. He had decided to join us

Friture

When my children were young we used to fish with a long, large net for tiny fish called whitebait or smelt. These tiny fish do not need to be cleaned, just patted dry with paper towels and dipped in a batter and fried. I served them inside a napkin with drinks. We ate them as if they were potato chips. The children loved them. This recipe is for 1 pound of bait. Place 1½ cups flour in a bowl or use rice flour for a lighter batter. Add 1 teaspoon salt, a pinch of pepper, 1 tablespoon melted butter, and 2 well-beaten eggs. Mix well and slowly add ¾ cup beer, stirring constantly. Refrigerate for 3 hours. Heat 4 cups vegetable oil. When the oil is hot, dip each bait into the batter and allow the excess to drip off. Fry several at a time until golden brown. Remove with a slotted spoon to a double layer of paper towels and keep the fish warm in a 275-degree oven while frying the remaining fish. Serve sprinkled with coarse salt. Serves 4.

in Hendaye for a week. I was in heaven. I went to the station to pick him up. "You are so brown" are the first words Jimmy said to me. "I am glad I came here." As we drove back to the hotel, Jimmy told me how beautiful Italy had been but he had had enough traveling for a while and wanted to swim and look around. For the next two days, we swam, lunched, swam again, dined, always in the company of my grandmother and brother. I was getting quite desperate. On the fourth day, Jimmy announced that he had caught a cold and was staying in bed. I was dispatched to bring him some chicken consommé. I quietly knocked at the door of his room, came in, and found him asleep. I put the soup on the table near his bed and looked at him sleeping. He was so handsome. I bent down and kissed him lightly. He grabbed my hand and kissed it. We both laughed. I sat on his bed and we talked. How to get rid of my brother, my grandmother, and be together, we asked each other. I had a brilliant idea: my grandmother was very vain and liked to flirt with men. An elderly gentleman staying at the hotel had befriended her. I said to Jimmy that I would go and talk to him and ask him to help us. I found him in the salon of the hotel and told him how I needed to be alone with Jimmy and how my grandmother never left us alone. He smiled and said he loved young lovers and he would take care of her. For the next few days he took my grandmother away on rides, visiting churches, and mainly flirting with her, which made her very happy. To get rid of my brother, Jimmy told him he wanted to sketch the small churches in the countryside, and that I would help him carry his watercolors. My brother, who preferred the beach and swimming, never came along. I followed Jimmy everywhere, watching him sketch the local fishermen, village scenes, and me. We talked about school, my mother, what I wanted to do after graduating from high school. Two days before Jimmy had to leave for Paris, we asked our old gentleman conspirator if we could go with him to Biarritz for the day. As we drove away with him, I suggested to Jimmy that we get off at La Negresse, a small village outside Biarritz, and wait there for him to pick us up. There was a lovely river with a small restaurant and we could easily spend time there. Mr. Arnold dropped us at La Negresse near a bridge over the small river. We walked to the edge and sat under a tree. Jimmy said nothing for a while, then turned to me and said, "Will you marry me?" I was silent for just a moment. "Of course I will marry you," I said, grinning wildly. "I love you!" We sat there in each other's arms for a while, then went across to the inn. I warned him, "Don't say anything to my grandmother! Wait until you are back in Paris and my mother will be there. We will tell her then." After lunch we went across the bridge to be picked up. Jimmy sat down on a stone and drew the hardware store on the other side of the little square, with its cowbells hanging on the doorway and lots of pots and pans and barrels on the floor. Today, the drawing is hanging in my bedroom.

That night Jimmy invited me to dinner at the local casino. I dressed up and we both went while my grandmother was taken to the theater by her new gentleman friend. The dinner was great, and for the only time in my life I don't remember what we ordered. When the bill came, Jimmy found that he did not have enough money, and I had none. Next door was a gambling room. I said to Jimmy, "Give me the money. I am always lucky at roulette. I will win!" He gave me all he had and followed me into the gambling room. I placed every last sou on numbers 5 and 13 and waited, my heart beating madly. The tiny ball stopped on the number 5! "I won, I won!" I cried in my excitement, forgetting that one does not scream upon winning in a casino. Someone tapped my shoulder. "Excuse me, miss. How old are you?" "Sixteen," I answered foolishly. "I am sorry. You cannot gamble! We will return the money you just bet." I was crushed and I explained in tears to the manager that we did not have enough money to pay the bill for our dinner and we were celebrating our engagement. He gave us back the money, paid the bill, and sent us back to our table with a bottle of champagne. What a wonderful evening!

The next day Jimmy left, promising to be back in Paris at the end of the month. A week later we returned to Paris. On September 15, Jimmy appeared in Paris and stayed with us. He would pick me up at school and we walked for hours together, planning the future. I called my mother and asked her to come and meet Jimmy.

As we all sat down in the living room, I proudly announced that Jimmy had proposed and that we were going to get married. Utter silence preceded an explosion. My grandmother said, "Never!" My mother said, "That's stupid! You are only sixteen, he has no profession, and he can't support you." My grandmother turned to Jimmy and continued her tirade. "How dare you! Under my roof! What would your mother say!" I was sobbing at this point, exaggerating the noise of my weeping and blowing my nose loudly. My mother suddenly said, in a loud, calm, imperious voice, "I have the solution. Colette, stop crying immediately! You must finish your baccalaureate, Jimmy must graduate from Harvard, and only then can he return. If you both feel the same as you do now, you can get married." Jimmy and I looked at each other and smiled. "Three years is nothing," I said. "I can wait."

This is the only time in my life that my mother took charge of me. For the next few days, we walked in Paris hand in hand. Jimmy promised to write very often and come back soon. The day he left I hugged and kissed him. "Don't forget me," I whispered. "I love you." For the next few months, letters came from America. First every week, then once a month, then a year later they stopped. I often prayed that he would not forget me. I talked about him with Claudine and sometimes my mother and my stepfather. They both would shake their heads and my stepfather would say, "Don't think about him too much. Go out with friends, have fun, and maybe he will come back." They both hoped that I would forget but I did not.

I had to wait three long years before he came back for me.

7

Summers

As *I turned seventeen,* I felt more sure of myself and started to take hold of my life. Since my mother was back now, my grandmother retreated to a more passive role. She still had her fake heart attacks whenever I went out or wanted to have friends in the house, but I ignored them. Another factor in my new independence was the fact that I passed the first part of my baccalaureate, *le bachot,* as the French call it, that spring. The *bachot* is the last exam taken before entering the university and is given over a two-year period. The second half of the exam concentrates on a specific strand of study or discipline, and students must choose which one they wish to pursue.

I was elated because I passed the exam with honors, just like my brother. *After all I am not that stupid,* I thought to myself. I had fallen in love with biology and had decided to take *sciences expérimentales,* which included literature and languages. Mentally I had planned it all: I would certainly apply to the Pasteur Institute, become a bacteriologist, and naturally win the Nobel Prize for my discoveries! I was proud, free, and for a very short period, independent.

Summer vacation in France is usually a family affair and mine was not different. This particular summer, however, I was determined to choose when and where I would go. Visiting Italy had been a long-term dream, and I often talked to Claudine about going with her to Rome and Venice. We planned out our trip and were about to tell her mother and my grandmother, when my grandmother announced a *conseil de famille* (family meeting). This felt ominous. Each time something important was to be decided, a *conseil de famille* took place during which my grandmother announced her intentions, my uncle Clément listened in silence, nodding in agreement, and I . . . well, I had nothing to say. If I disagreed or objected, my grandmother told me in no uncertain terms to do what I was told and to shut up.

Clément arrived at our house that Saturday morning, and I was astonished to hear him thank my grandmother for receiving him. I had been wrong after all; she did not call for the *conseil de famille. He* did! Well, I thought, *this should be interesting. I wonder what he wants from her?* As they chitchatted for a few minutes, my mind was racing; *could he, by any wild chance, help me to get away from this household?*

Clément's voice interrupted my reverie, and I listened in shock to what he was saying, bluntly, firmly, in his strangely feminine voice. "She is seventeen, Rose . . . I think she should come with me and Germaine to Cannes this summer. She should get married soon and there we can introduce her to some young men of good family . . ." I stopped listening. *Get married? Didn't he understand that I wanted to finish my studies? That I wanted to marry Jimmy?* (I had just gotten a letter from Jimmy telling me how much he was enjoying Harvard.) *And going to Cannes with them! Oh my God . . . there goes Italy. At least I won't be with her.*

My grandmother looked annoyed but said nothing for a moment. "When will you go?" she finally asked with a frown. "The last two weeks in July and the whole month of August. She will need clothes," Clément added, handing my grandmother a check. "They should be elegant but understated." Later I over-heard her complain to one of her friends that she was not going on vacation in August with us after all. I understood then that my grandmother lived on the money we paid her every month. Vacation was paid for her if and when she took us with her. My grandmother had very little money of her own. My grandfather, who had been a very wealthy businessman, had placed his money in a secret account in Switzerland. But I had heard rumors that my grandfather had refused to give his wife the number of his account. After the war she had sold most of her jewelry to live but she owned the apartment on Avenue de la Grande Armée and she had made an arrangement with Clément. She would take care of both of us in exchange for a monthly stipend. She often forgot that we were paying her and sometimes complained of how much money we were costing her, with a special emphasis on what I was costing her.

For the next few weeks we ran from store to store buying bathing suits (one-piece), summer dresses, sandals, and one long evening dress for *une soirée,* my grandmother said. Needless to say, she failed to buy me anything elegant, except for my evening gown. At this point I was getting used to the idea of Cannes. When Claudine heard that our jaunt to Italy was called off, she smiled, hiding her disappointment. "I know you'll have a wonderful time. Just don't flirt too much. Before you leave, Colette, how about spending a few days with me in the country?"

Clément and Germaine left two weeks later for Cannes. Clément let me know that he expected me August first. *"Sois sage entre temps"* (Be good meanwhile), he warned me. At Claudine's invitation I went with her to her country house in Monford l'Amaury, about one hour from Paris. It was quite a fashionable little town where artists and writers had summerhouses. There was one two-star restaurant, an old church, the post office, the town hall, and a café where the youth of the town would gather. Claudine's house was slightly outside the village. I loved that house. It was a two-story, seventeenth-century French country estate with a very high stone wall surrounding it and a large garden in the back. The living room was my favorite space. Its tall French windows opened onto the garden, and in the morning the sun filtered through the high *persiennes* (shutters) and formed patterns on the old-fashioned Victorian furniture. Every day, buried in a deep, faded pink armchair just wide enough for one person, sat Claudine's tragic mother reading a book. A tiny, thin woman with gray-white hair pulled back into a chignon, she always had a faraway look and a wan smile. She hardly ever conversed but always had a kind word for me. She got up from her chair for lunch and afterward took a walk around the garden. She sank into the armchair again until dinnertime; in the evening, after urging us to go out, she retired to her room for the night. She and I talked about the garden, for which she felt a great attachment. Her husband had designed it and had planted it with espalier peach and pear trees against the walls, rose bushes in the center. At the back end of the garden was a vegetable patch planted with young lettuces, tomatoes, string beans, and artichokes. I had never seen an artichoke plant before, and during these two weeks, I went every day to see if there were any growing. On the last day I saw a tiny one and picked it. Claudine was appalled, explaining that I shouldn't touch them that young and that Alice, the cook, would be upset with me. Panicking, I gobbled it up raw. The artichoke tasted bitter but I didn't want to upset Alice at any cost. I loved being in the kitchen watching her cook. She had been with Claudine's family for decades and was devoted to them. Seeing that Claudine and I were best friends, she also took me in. Although Alice was dour and seldom smiled, she made me feel at home. The kitchen was rustic: in order to wash dishes, she had to heat the water in a woodburning stove. I was fascinated by this stove. I carefully watched Alice's thin, sinewy arms lift the steel disks on top of the range to add more wood. The flames jumped up at her, but she always managed to avoid being singed. Then there was the table—a long, thick marble slab on which Alice would make her famous tarts. I have since developed an automatic response to compare the tart I am eating to her perfect ones from long ago. Shimmering raspberries, like garnets in the summer sun, sitting on delicate *crème anglaise* and a barely sweetened, tender crust. Never since have I tasted such fruity splendor in a dessert.

Alice's Raspberry Tart

Make the pâte brisée: *In a bowl place ½ cup chilled butter and 3 tablespoons vegetable shortening. Add 2 cups flour, ½ teaspoon salt, and 2 tablespoons sugar and work the flour and the butter together. Slowly add 5 tablespoons cold water and mix well until it forms an elastic dough. Wrap in foil and refrigerate for 2 hours or more. Butter a 9-inch pie pan. On a floured board roll the dough about one-eighth of an inch thick. Line the pie pan with the dough, pressing the edges with a fork. Fill the pie pan with dry beans. Bake the dough in a preheated 325-degree oven for 30 minutes. Remove from the oven, remove the beans, and allow to cool at room temperature. Meanwhile make the* crème anglaise. *In the top of a double boiler placed over simmering water mix together ½ cup heavy cream, 5 beaten egg*

yolks, ⅔ cup sugar, and a pinch of salt. Stir con-
stantly until the cream thickens. Remove from
the heat and cool. Add 1 tablespoon good
cognac (optional). Spread the cream on the bot-
tom of the cooked pie. Hull 2 cups ripe raspber-
ries and sprinkle the fruit with 2 tablespoons
very fine sugar and 1 tablespoon lime juice.
Toss and set aside for 10 minutes. Arrange the
raspberries in concentric circles on top of the
cream. In a small saucepan heat ½ cup seedless
raspberry jelly until it is liquefied. With a pas-
try brush, brush the raspberry jelly on the
raspberries. Cool at room temperature and
serve. Serves 6.

The cupboards were bursting with jars of jams and preserves.
Alice called us to the kitchen, where she had been brewing her
confiture aux quatre fruits. "Taste it," she barked. "Do you think
it's sweet enough?" We scooped up some of the just-cooled
jam—made with strawberries, raspberries, and red and black
currants—from the marble and licked every finger. "It's perfect!"
we shouted in unison. No smile was proffered, but her small
black eyes softened.

On the weekend, friends of the family came for lunch. Alice
often made a roast leg of lamb she called *le gigot qui pleure* (the
leg of lamb that cries) because the fat from the meat would fall
onto the small potatoes—soft and golden and redolent of garlic—that surrounded it. On Sunday it was always a *jambon per-*

Le Gigot Qui Pleure

This dish is usually made in the spring or summer with young lamb. In a food processor, mince 3 garlic cloves with 2 tablespoons fresh rosemary, 4 tablespoons butter, and salt and pepper. With a knife remove the paper outer covering of a 4- to 5-pound leg of lamb. Peel 3 more garlic cloves and insert sliver of garlic all over the meat. Rub the meat with the mixture of butter, garlic, and rosemary. The lamb should be covered all over with the butter. Preheat the oven to 450 degrees. Grease a large roasting pan with olive oil and place the meat on a rack in the roasting pan. Peel 32 small white potatoes and place them around the meat inside the roasting pan. Bake for 5 minutes, lower the heat to 325 degrees, and bake 15 minutes per pound for rare and 20 minutes per pound for pink. Stir the potatoes from time to time so that they brown on all sides. When the meat is done, remove to a platter with the potatoes. Pour all the liquid from the pan into a glass jar and remove half the fat. Pour the liquid back into the pan and add 1 cup chicken stock, salt and pepper to taste, and 1 tablespoon fresh tarragon. Carve the meat and pour some of the sauce over it. Serves 6 to 8.

sillé, a ham stuffed with parsley and garlic in a light jelly. She served it with home-grown braised leeks and tomato salad. My favorite of her dishes was *poussin à l'estragon,* a far cry from my grandmother's tough chicken. The tiny birds were stuffed with fresh tarragon, butter, and soft bread, and roasted until their skin was crisp and the meat moist and tender.

In the evenings, Claudine and I walked to the village, sat in a café, and talked about our future. Claudine wanted to meet religious Jews and had befriended a young couple with children. "I want you to meet them," she said. "You'll see what being Jewish really means." By then I had told Claudine about my convent days and how difficult it was to live as both a Catholic and a Jew. I really did not know how to give an answer to that request. I had, in the past year, become very much aware of what had happened during the war: the concentration camps, the death of six million Jews, the attitude of some of the French, and especially the stories that went around about the Catholic church and the Pope. I was torn between my Jewish heritage—which I knew nothing about but heard every day from my grandmother, who kept on saying, "You are a Jew, whether you like it or not"—and my profound faith in Catholicism. When thing were too difficult I closed my eyes and transported myself to the small chapel in Cairo in the Convent of the Sacred Heart, where I had spent such wonderful years. The chapel was small, with a large reproduction of Botticelli's Madonna. She looked so peaceful and kind. Young brides would come after their wedding and drop their bouquets of flowers on the altar. Very often as a

Poussin à l'Estragon
(Baby Chicken with Tarragon)

Poussins are very young chickens. They are available in most gourmet stores that sell poultry. To make this dish the way Alice made it, the poussins have to be prepared two days in advance. Rinse and pat dry 4 poussins. Fill the cavities with paper towels and place them, uncovered, in the refrigerator for two days. This step will allow the skin breast to dry and keep the moisture in the chicken when cooking. Mix 8 tablespoons softened butter with 4 tablespoons tarragon and salt and freshly ground pepper. Slip the butter mixture under the breast's skin. Rub the exterior of the poussins with butter. Place inside the cavity 1 tablespoon cream cheese and 1 to 2 tablespoons chopped fresh tarragon. Sprinkle the poussins with coarse salt and place them on a rack in a roasting pan. Add ½ cup chicken broth to the pan and bake the poussins in a preheated 350-degree oven for 45 minutes, or until they are golden brown. Remove the poussins to a serving platter and garnish with watercress or cilantro. Degrease the pan juices, adding more broth if necessary. Serve the juice along with the poussins and mashed potatoes. Serves 4.

child I went and prayed there. Today, at seventeen, I could with no problem, go to church on Sunday but I didn't. I was no longer a Catholic nor was I a Jew. Who I was had not been discovered yet. There was no one kind enough around me to understand what I felt. Jewish holidays were the worst for me. My grandmother, who had not practiced her religion in years, and prided herself on not looking like a Jew, suddenly became religious as soon as she found out about Mother and me. She did not talk to me about it, but there was this silence whenever a religious holiday came to pass. Sometimes I followed her to a temple but I could never feel that this is where I belonged.

I looked at Claudine who was waiting for an answer from me. I promised her that when I came back from Cannes I would go and visit her friends. I never did.

We also talked about our last year in high school and shared our imagined futures. Despite the fact that Jimmy had written to me only a few times, I was sure, I told Claudine, that he'd come back and marry me. I left the human warmth of Monford for a very different warmth in Cannes, one that emanated not from my hosts but only from the sun.

During the war Cannes had been a haven for many people, Jews and non-Jews alike, trying to escape the German invasion and to live under Pétain's "free" France (which was hardly free at all). Clément and other members of my family had escaped to Cannes. They all had Egyptian passports and were never touched by the French militia or the German Gestapo. After the war, by the time I joined Clément in Cannes, the city had regained its splendor and had become the center of the new cinema. The Carlton Palace was an enormous white hotel, built in the early 1920s on the *croisette* (boardwalk). It was separated from the road by a magnificent garden filled with exotic plants and palm trees. I arrived early in the morning and went in search of Clément and Germaine. I was told that Clément took his breakfast on the terrace of his room and would be down around eleven. Germaine never rose before noon. Meanwhile I had to fend for myself. My room was small with a balcony overlooking the back garden. Netting surrounded the bed, and the boy who brought up my luggage told me that Cannes had lots of mosquitoes. "You must be sure to sleep under the net," he said, standing at the door, waiting. What was he waiting for? Then I understood. *God,* I thought, *I don't know how much to give him! Why didn't Clément meet me?* I looked in my bag for change and handed him a five-franc coin. He glanced at it with vague disgust and left abruptly. *I was wrong! I gave him too little. Well, I don't care. I never wanted to be here in the first place!*

I went for a walk on the *croisette.* Young women in small bikinis were walking up and down, looking beautiful; older women with young men were doing the same. On the beach under umbrellas, women were sunning themselves, bare-chested. *I could never do that,* I thought, *never.* By eleven o'clock I was starving, having had no breakfast. I walked down some backstreets and found a tiny pastry shop with an Italian name selling croissants, small sandwiches filled with ham, pastries, and coffee. I sat down and asked for a strong cup of coffee. What was

placed in front of me was a small cup topped with what seemed
to be a white foamy cloud of milk. I gulped it down and was
surprised by its aromatic, slightly bitter taste. "What is it?" I
asked the young waitress. *"Espresso machiato,"* she answered
with a smile. "It's Italian." At that moment I knew for certain
that I was hooked for life on *machiatos.* I ordered the small sand
wich that she called *panino,* a light, slightly sweet brioche-type
roll filled with prosciutto. I ate two of them with gusto and was
about to order a third one when I heard my grandmother's voice
in my head saying, "You are too fat!" I paid and left the café,
pleased with myself that I had resisted the temptation. Every
morning for the next few weeks, I avoided the hotel's stuffy *salle
à manger* and went to Luigi's for my breakfast, an excursion
away from my family that became the highlight of my day.

At noon I met Clément and Germaine in the lobby.
Germaine was a tall, top-heavy woman with beautiful legs.
Her face was greasy with streaks of cream, and I dreaded kissing her in the morning but she insisted, and I walked away
with the taste of face cream on my lips. On the first morning
she wore a lovely navy blue halter top over a sweeping white
shirt and an immense hat that covered her gray hair. She hated
the sun and hardly ever took off her oversize sunglasses. The
three of us crossed the *croisette* toward the beach club, where
Clément had rented a cabana for the summer. The club also
had a restaurant, and usually by two o'clock we were sitting
there surrounded by their friends, mostly Parisians. Once in a
while one of them brought along a son, and he was seated near

me. It was impossible to talk, being surrounded by older people, dulled from their leisure and excess. I wasn't interested anyway, and I'd excuse myself as the dessert came. I'd go for walks on the boardwalk or take the bus to Nice, which I loved. I was expected back by dinner, usually a formal affair at an elegant restaurant. I ordered *langoustines* with fresh basil or *pigeonneau,* a small squab, wrapped in lettuce leaves. Even if I liked the food, I couldn't bear sitting in restaurants, utterly bored.

One night Clément told me to put on my evening dress since we were going to dinner at La Palme d'Or, a two-star restaurant. He had once again invited some Parisian friends and their son. I liked the idea of dressing up but not of meeting yet another prospective suitor who probably hated the idea as much as I. Just before leaving my room, I looked at myself in the mirror and liked what I saw. The pale green dress made my brown skin glow and showed how small my waist was. I had put some makeup on and darkened my eyelashes. I looked Egyptian, and my eyes seemed to be filled with light. Feeling charmed, I went downstairs to meet them. Germaine gave me a look of approval and Clément took my arms, saying, "What a lovely young girl! You will charm them all tonight." As we entered the restaurant in the lobby of the Hôtel Martinez, I spotted a tall young man with dark hair swept away from his face and an exceptionally long, aquiline nose. I was introduced to Francis Levi and his parents, and I was seated next to him. He was rather sullen during dinner and spoke little. I managed to learn that he had been accepted at the Polytechnique, the prestigious French school of social sciences, and had a great future in front of him—or at least this is what his parents proclaimed. After dinner, I was astonished when Francis asked me out for the next day. I acquiesced only because I had nothing else to do and because Clément gave me one of his looks. Francis intrigued me. He lacked charm and was not adept at conversation, but he was willing to be ordered about. Over the next few days, I made him drive me to Nice and Monte Carlo, take me to lunch, and take me to avant-garde movies, which he disliked. After a week he announced that he had to leave Cannes and go back to Paris. I was sorry to see him go. I did not like him much, but he offered me an escape and seemed to enjoy simply following me around. For the next two years Francis called me from time to time, to take me out to dinner in expensive restaurants, and to the Opera Ball every year. One summer, a dozen years later, I spotted his parents in the Jardin de Luxembourg in Paris. My children were watching an open-air puppet show. I approached them with a smile and reminded them of who I was; I was astonished by his mother's anger in response. "You ruined my son's life," she screamed. "He loved you and you pushed him away. He went to Africa and married a black woman. I hate you!" He loved me? He had never said a word to me, never showed me any affection, but I felt guilty just the same remembering all the places I had made him take me.

After Francis's departure, I was stifled yet again by the boring routine of my summer vacation. I wrote to my stepfather to ask him if I could come and spend the rest of August in Chatelguyon, where he was staying. He acquiesced, and Clément and Germaine were pleased to see me go. Trying to marry me off had backfired, and there were no more young men around who seemed to like me.

Chatelguyon had been well known for its waters, which, it was said, would cure most stomach ailments and arthritis. During the war the town had fallen on bad times and had deteriorated. After the war my stepfather and his partners bought several of the hotels dirt cheap, and Mira started a campaign to make Chatelguyon a center of haute cuisine. Every one of his hotels boasted a two-star chef, and by the time I joined them, the town had recovered some of its past luster. The town also had a small casino, and every afternoon, with twenty-five francs in my pocket, I bet at the roulette table. Because I was not yet twenty-one, my stepfather had made an arrangement with the casino to let me bet in the afternoon. I discovered that I loved gambling—the rush it gave me. I also liked the olives and slices of *saucisson sec* they served at the end of the gambling session. Often in the evening Mira took my mother and me to Clermont-Ferrand, a large town about twenty kilometers from Chatelguyon, to explore the local restaurants. I still remember some of the dishes I ate, perhaps because they were unusual: rooster sausage cooked in red wine, pigeon stuffed with pork, and my favorites, pig cheek and snout in a velvety sauce, and braised pears in cognac. Mira and I compared notes and discussed the complexities of preparation, balance, and composition. I began to enjoy myself and even got along with my mother, for the first and only time in my life. She was busy taking the waters, talking with her friends about all her ailments, and being as motherly as she possibly could to me. Sometimes I couldn't stand her complaints and made fun of them, certain that she was exaggerating the pains in her legs or back. Today I feel sorry about my callousness, and angry with myself for not being more concerned about her health while she was alive. I too have arthritis in my legs, and some days I really feel the pain and think of her.

I returned to Paris and my usual routine, but now my grandmother and I were no longer on speaking terms. I still had to ask permission to go out, and at least once a month, she developed a *crise cardiaque* just as I left to be with friends. The doctor would arrive, examine her briefly, and proclaim that all she needed was a bit of rest. (She certainly was all right, and she lived without major illness until the age of 92!) The year was uneventful. School was challenging, but I wanted to succeed so I worked very hard and in July passed my *bachot*. High school was over and I could go to the Pasteur Institute in the fall.

But what about the summer? There was no way I was going anywhere with my grandmother or Clément or my mother. One day I saw an advertisement asking for a French teacher for a school in England. The headmaster was coming to Paris to interview prospective teachers. I recognized an opportunity and wrote a letter asking for an interview. An answer arrived a few days later, setting an appointment for the second week in July. I was excited at the prospect of having a job. But I had one problem. The ad had mentioned that the job required teachers to be at least twenty years old. I had just turned eighteen and looked about fifteen. My hair was in braids, I wore no makeup, and I was short! For the interview I simply *had* to look older. Claudine was no help; she looked like me, so I turned to the sophisticated and worldly Nicole, who introduced me to a model whom her brother represented. Martine thought it would be fun to transform me into a Parisian sophisticate. She lent me clothes (which I managed to squeeze into) and high-heeled shoes, and she took me to her hairdresser for a more fashionable hairdo. On the day of the interview, she applied my makeup. By the time she had finished, I looked twenty-five, serious, and very sophisticated. It was no surprise to me that I got the job, which was to teach French to young boys whose parents were out of the country. I was to leave for Brighton at the end of the month for a one-month stay. The pay was decent and the headmaster was supposed to be quite genial. Now I had to tell my grandmother and my uncle what I had decided to do. My grandmother said nothing when I made my announcement. She was going to New York to see her family and did not seem to care. Clément's reaction took me by surprise. He was angry with me. He said how terrible it was to work for a school at my age; what would people say? That we had lost our money? I would never get married, he moaned bitterly. This was terrible. But I refused to give in and responded that I was going to work in August and nothing would make me change my mind.

On August first I took the train to Calais and from Calais the boat to Dover and then another train to Brighton. The headmaster was waiting for me at the station. Upon seeing me he looked crestfallen and said in an angry voice, "This won't do . . . no, this won't do!" I was confused. "You look too young," he explained, shaking his head. "These boys are sixteen, seventeen years old. You were supposed to be housed in their dormitory building, but I can't let it happen. You'll have to stay with us." I suddenly realized that I hadn't looked the same when we first met. I apologized and said that I would buy shoes with heels and use makeup. I admitted that I was only eighteen and insisted that I could teach well. Everything, I promised him, would be fine.

The headmaster's wife wasn't too pleased to see me. I was given a small room on the top floor of their house. That night at dinner I realized that for the next few weeks I had to forget about eating. Mrs. Charington could not cook. Her roast beef was brown through and through, her vegetables overcooked, and her desserts heavy. But the next morning, I found breakfast to be a revelation. I was served broiled kippers—salty, smoky, and slathered with butter—thick slabs of toasted bread, and very strong English tea. Breakfast became my only sensuous pleasure. I loved the steamed haddock, the fresh, soft-boiled eggs, and the hearty porridge. Luckily, I ate my fill in the morning; lunch and dinner simply offered me the challenge of hiding the fact that I did not eat them. In four weeks I lost fifteen pounds! I was sure that when I went back to Paris no one would recognize me, and my grandmother could no longer call me fat. I quickly gained the reputation of being a difficult Frenchwoman. Mr. Charington was sorry that he had hired me.

The morning after my arrival, following her husband's command, Mrs. Charington took me shopping. We bought high-heeled shoes, dark red lipstick, rouge, and combs to put my long hair up. Once made up and dressed to kill, I was sent to teach the young boys French. Over the next four weeks I found out that I loved teaching, that I was good at it. I felt like an actress performing on a stage, and my audience was not only enjoying themselves, but also learning French. The boys asked me questions about France, girls, French kisses, food, and how to say "I love you" in French. They wrote me poems that they used to slip in with their homework, and gave me small gifts. I loved it. Evenings, of course, were less pleasurable since I couldn't go out without facing the headmaster's wrath. But I was happy—I had proved to myself that I could work and earn a living.

Back in Paris in September, I registered at the Pasteur Institute to start what I believed would be a successful career in bacteriology. I was assigned to a Russian doctor who was studying rare blood diseases. My role in the beginning was to draw blood every morning from three goats and in the afternoon to work in the national French hospital for the poor. Little did I know that this setup would bring about a final break with my grandmother and change my life forever.

8

The Break

T*he Pasteur Institute,* unlikely as it may seem, became a welcome refuge, and I was happy. Occupying two acres in the 15th arrondissement, the institute had a forbidding aspect. A high wall of faded reddish brick surrounded the multi-structured complex, including a barn where the goats and other animals were kept. Students' assignments, in three-month intervals, were determined by lottery. I drew the hematology department first and was assigned to Dr. R., a Russian woman in her fifties with a thick accent. She was heavily made up, and her dyed curly blond hair was held on top of her head by a wide comb. I enjoyed listening to her swear in Russian whenever one of her curls loosened from the comb, which was often. She was trying to find cures for certain blood diseases in young children. My job the first week was to mount the billy goats and draw blood. At first I was clumsy and my white lab coat was more often than not covered with blood. Dr. R. clucked benignly each time I returned to the lab, where I assisted her in preparing slides. I had lunch at home and then walked to the hospital, where I had afternoon duty, drawing blood again, this time from children. The métro ride home from the institute was pleasant, at least for me. Inevitably, a void was created around me—I smelled to high heaven of goat—and I could sit down in the crowded métro car and read my book or my notes. At home the problem of my bloody doctor's coat became quite an issue. The coat had to be washed daily, and soon our housekeeper simply refused. The other problem was my grandmother. She made me eat lunch in the kitchen. "*Tu empeste* (You stink)!" she'd say in a disgusted tone. I felt like Cinderella but I liked my job. Soon Dr. R. taught me how to make slides, to draw what I saw in the microscope, and to count cells. I was looking forward to starting my studies for real, and hematology was a compelling field. Every week, Clément got an earful of complaints about me from my grandmother. "Who will ever marry her," she told him. "Is this really what *une jeune fille de bonne famille* should be doing?" Clément tried to dissuade me from my studies, but I was resolute. Money was also becoming a real problem. When my father died, he left his fortune to be managed by his eldest brother, my uncle Albert. Egyptian law, however, was very strict about children's inheritance. The government had created a department that was responsible for managing the child's portion of all inheritances. It determined how much the child needed, and every month a check was deposited in the child's account. This was done to protect the child, especially the male child, from a new marriage or an unscrupulous relative. An auditor, to be paid by the estate, was assigned to each account. When Nasser took over the government, exiling King Farouk, he ordered a review of all the orphans' accounts. At this point, the new government declared that our family's accountant had been underpaid for the last ten years and that adjustments had to be made. My uncle Albert decided that we should contest the finding. While the money trickled pitifully in, Clément was obliged to support both my brother and me, since these funds were so paltry. Marrying me off was the perfect solution. And so the rounds of prospective husbands resumed. Every eligible young man whose parents were friends of my family or even friends of a friend was paraded before my eyes. I disliked them all, including a pompous Rothschild in whom my grandmother put all her hopes, though I did enjoy—and take advantage of— dining out at fancy restaurants, dancing at clubs, and attending the latest plays and musicals. After several months, an incident at work solved Clément and my grandmother's problem.

Students at Pasteur were told that they were going to need a physical and a tuberculosis vaccine. A few days after I had the vaccine I developed a fever, my arm swelled, and I felt quite sick. I called Dr. R., who immediately came to see me and sent me to have an X ray of my lungs. The results came a few days later; I had a touch of tuberculosis and had to be sent immediately to a mountain retreat for a few months. I protested, so Dr. R. came up with an attractive solution. She had Russian friends who lived outside Megève in a lovely old chalet; the husband was a retired doctor who agreed to take care of me. Within two days, to my grandmother's relief, I was packed off to the Alps and Dr. and Mrs. Alexandrov.

The chalet was a two-story wooden house filled with mementos from Russia. In the living room, photographs of the entire family in ornate silver frames were placed on every piece of heavy, velvet-upholstered furniture. Mrs. Alexandrov, Tania to her friends, was a short, round, bosomy lady who greeted me with warmth. "I will take care of you," she said in a heavy Russian accent. "Bubbola, don't you worry about anything." Dr. Alexandrov resembled my grandfather, with a white mustache and a shock of white hair. I liked him immensely. "You like opera?" he asked. "Yes, I do," I responded politely. Immediately, the doctor jumped out of his seat. "I know Caruso. I have all his records," he exclaimed as he placed a record on the player. I was enchanted. Today, whenever I listen to my CDs of Caruso, I remember my stay with the Alexandrovs. I was taken upstairs to my bedroom and ordered to rest until dinnertime. Unlike the stuffy downstairs living room, my bedroom was white-washed, with large windows overlooking the mountains and an old-fashioned four-poster bed with lots of pillows and the thickest eiderdown I had ever seen. As I lay down to rest, Caruso's voice drifted up, and slowly I went to sleep. The days passed very quickly: I ate breakfast—thick slices of black bread slathered with fresh butter, hot cocoa—then a short walk. I rested again, had lunch, rested again, another short walk, and dinner. At night they told me stories about Russia, and Tania proudly showed me photographs of herself as a young girl in a ball gown. She described the balls in the winter in Saint Petersburg with a quivering voice. They had escaped in 1920 after the revolution and settled in Paris. They ran a small restaurant for the other Russian émigrés. Tania was an excellent cook, and very soon the restaurant became quite famous. Dr. Alexandrov was never allowed to practice in France, but he took care of all his Russian friends. When they retired, he bought the chalet in the mountains and took in guests in the winter and summer. Once in a while Dr. R. would send him a patient like me. I loved Tania's food, especially her borscht. She often served it at the midday meal, followed by a red-and-white radish salad or some mushrooms in cream. At dinner we had flounder with scallions, shashlik with kasha, potatoes and green peppers stuffed with carrots. There were a lot of sweet desserts that I did not care for, so Tania always gave me fruit compote served with sweet cream. On Sundays we ate blinis with sour cream, and I could wolf down at least half a dozen. I gained weight and looked very healthy. No one in my family came to see me during these months but I did not care, as I loved being pampered by the Alexandrovs. Within four months Dr. Alexandrov decided that I was in good shape, and with tears in their eyes, the tender couple sent me back to my grandmother.

Blinis

*This recipe takes time but it is worth the
wait. Pour 1¼ cups of very warm water into a
bowl. Add 1 package active dry yeast and mix
well until the yeast is all dissolved. Add ¾ cup
flour and mix well, cover, and allow to stand on
the side of the range for about 3 hours. Then
add 1¼ cups buckwheat flour, mix well, and let
stand for about 1½ hours. Heat 1 cup milk; add
the milk to the flour mixture, and beat the mixture with a hand beater. Beat 2 egg yolks with a
pinch of salt and 1 teaspoon sugar until light
yellow. Gradually beat 2 tablespoons melted
butter into the egg mixture, add to the flour
mixture, and mix well. Then beat until stiff 2
egg whites with a pinch of salt. Fold in ¼ cup
heavy cream. Then fold the egg whites into the
flour mixture, and let stand for about 1½ hours.
Butter a skillet and drop tablespoons of the batter onto the skillet. When the blinis are brown
on one side, pour a little melted butter on top
and flip the blinis. Cook until that side is
brown. Serve the blinis with sour cream, caviar,
or smoked salmon. Makes about 25 blinis.*

As I entered my bedroom in our house in Paris, I saw two letters on my dresser, one of which was stamped with the Pasteur
Institute's logo. I was afraid to open them, sensing that they con-
tained bad news. The letter from Pasteur stated that they could

not take me back by order of the government. I was crushed; I had worked so hard for nothing. The other letter, from the Ministry of Education, explained that the funds for my studies at the institute were being withdrawn. I had become a risk, and the government no longer wanted to foot the bill for my recovery. I could, like other students living in Paris, go to the Sorbonne at their expense but not to Pasteur. I sat on my bed, feeling cursed, damned, jinxed. Everything I wanted was always taken away. As I stared at the walls of my bedroom through my tears, I knew I could no longer stay in that house. I had to go out on my own, but where? My mother's house was out of the question. She had made it clear that she wanted to be alone with her new husband. I called Clément to tell him what happened. "Wonderful!" he gloated. "You can now act like a real young lady should and choose something more in keeping with who you are." Who I was? I had no clue and felt inconsequential. All I knew was that I could not expect any help from him except in the form of money. "You must come and see me tomorrow. We will have lunch together and discuss your future." As I hung up the telephone I looked up, and there was my grandmother, imperiously glaring. "You are not going back to the institute," she said with relief. "Thank goodness . . . it took weeks to get rid of the goat smell in your room!" Without a single word to console me, she departed. I left the house and went for a walk on the Avenue de la Grande Armée, a majestic, tree-lined path to the Arc de Triomphe. The arch was illuminated, shimmering against a backdrop of violet dusk, and I remembered the day I had seen it for the first time. I was eager then to start a life with my "real" family. But three years later, I was alone. I stood near the arch for a long time, looking at cars passing by, people coming home from work, young women hanging on the arms of their boyfriends. I finally returned to my room, refused supper, and cried myself to sleep.

The next day at lunch (I could not stay away from food for long), while I was enjoying a velvety onion soup topped with a layer of melted Gruyère, Clément threw a bombshell at my feet. "I am sending you to Egypt," he said. "You have to go there. Albert is contesting the government's edict about accountant fees and they need you in Cairo." I would have been thrilled by his proclamation two years ago, but now my grandparents were dead and I wanted to stay in Paris, to study or to work. "I don't want to go," I said in a self-assured voice that surprised me. "I want to register at the Sorbonne and take a degree in . . ." What did I want to study? I really didn't know. ". . . English and literature," I finished, thinking of Jimmy in America. Although I had not heard from him in more than a year, I knew I had to learn English. "It is only until the summer," he explained. "Next fall you can go to school if you still want to. Now go back home and pack your bags and all your belongings. I will give you a studio in one of my apartment buildings. Leave them there and go to Cairo." I looked at my uncle in astonishment. *What had happened? He was actually going to let me live on my own?* I decided not to ask but to do what he told me and quickly move out of the house. "You will leave in a week. I bought the ticket; this time you fly." With sudden gusto, I gobbled down my veal chop stuffed with herbs and devoured a *tarte Tatin.*

That evening, I announced to my grandmother that I was moving out. *"Une chambre de bonne avec salle de bains* (a maid's room with a bathroom)," I said proudly. My grandmother was lying in bed, and I stood at the foot, thinking how wonderful it was going to be to leave her oppressive presence. Out of the blue, she spoke harshly. *"Pars! Tu reviendras car tu finiras sur le trottoir avec un gosse*

Onion Soup

Peel and thinly slice 4 large sweet onions. In a large skillet melt 1 tablespoon butter with 1 tablespoon olive oil. Add the onions and sauté over medium heat, stirring often. When the onions are light brown, add 6 cups chicken or beef broth and simmer the onions for another 5 minutes. Correct the seasoning, adding salt and pepper. Toast 4 thick slices of country bread. Divide the soup among 4 earthenware soup bowls. Cut 4 slices of Gruyère into ½-inch pieces and divide the cheese among the bowls. Place a slice of toast in each bowl. Put 1 or 2 slices of Gruyère on top of the soup. Dot the cheese with a small piece of butter and bake in a preheated 375-degree oven for 10 minutes, or until the cheese is golden brown and bubbly. Serve immediately. Serves 4.

sur le bras ou à l'Assistance Publique (Leave! You'll come back, since you'll end up walking the streets with a kid in your arms or on welfare)." I took it as a challenge and vowed to myself that I'd be *good,* so that no one would speak ill of me.

As I was packing my clothes and my few belongings, my brother came in. "Why are you doing this?" he asked. "I know it is difficult here but you just have to stand it for one more year. You know she has a lot of diamonds, and they will be yours one day. She told me." "Diamonds?" I said. "You can have them. I'm leaving."

My studio was on the eighth floor of a very elegant building on the Avenue Foch. The room was small with one window, a tiny bathroom, a bed, a desk, and a chair. Clément was there with me to introduce me to the concierge. Concierges in France are the queens of dwellings. They control the mail, know who comes in and out, and keep abreast of all the gossip about each tenant. This concierge was to look after me, meaning, I understood, to report to Clément what I was doing, where I went, and especially who came to the attic to visit. I knew I had to behave; if not, this small studio would be taken from me and I would end up like Cinderella for real, back at the hearth. My first night there I slept like a log.

I flew to Cairo a week later. The noise from the crowds at the airport was almost deafening, and soldiers with guns were milling about everywhere. I had to wait endlessly on the customs line, and when it was my turn, the customs officer looked at my French passport and asked me to follow him. I was taken to a small room where two policemen were sitting at a table. "Why do you have a French passport?" I was asked in Arabic. "I don't understand Arabic," I answered in French. "You don't, but your family is Egyptian. What happened to you?" I tried to explain that my Arabic was poor, that I had been living in France, and that my mother was French. They finally let me go. Outside, trembling, I was accosted several times by men in dirty clothes offering me rides in a taxi and hotel rooms. I finally spotted my cousin, who pushed everyone aside, grabbed me by the arm, and took me to his car. Egypt was now ruled by Nasser. Soldiers were everywhere in the streets, and traffic was abominable. Cairo had changed since I'd left; there seemed to be more people in the streets than before. We passed a new, enormous building. "It's the new police headquarters," my cousin explained with a sigh. "Life has been more difficult since the revolution. Lots of people have left. Government is chaotic now and rules change every day."

The house was there, as lovely as I remembered, with red and white bougainvillea growing on the fence. Mohammed, the protector of the house (the house, my cousin explained, needed protection from the mob that now roamed the streets), greeted me with arms waving and a huge toothless smile. As I entered my grandparents' apartments I was suddenly filled with sadness. I had been so happy here with them, but now my uncle Albert and his wife were living in their apartment. They greeted me warmly, and soon I felt more at ease. My room was unchanged, and from the balcony I could still touch the mango tree that my grandfather said he had planted when I was born. Then I drifted toward the kitchen. Ahmet our cook was still there. As I looked at him, I remembered how wonderful he had been to me. When my mother left me with my grandparents, Ahmet had taken me into his kitchen. He had adopted me, and whenever I was lonely or sad he had always found a way to cheer me up. When I was a young child he would plop me on the marble counter and give me the spoon filled with the chocolate mousse he was making or, behind my grandmother's back (she objected to a *jeune fille de bonne famille* in the kitchen), he would fill a small pita with hot *ful medamas* that he made for the kitchen staff. Today, he looked older and thinner but his smile was as warm as I remembered it. He hugged me and told me I looked beautiful but too thin. He would cook for me all the dishes he remembered I liked. I was home! I promised myself that this time I would ask him to teach me how to prepare some of his dishes, like his broiled quail stuffed vine leaves and pickled garlic. This time I knew I could help him in the kitchen. I realized very quickly that things were not the same. When I was a child, there were many servants, chauffeurs, and gardeners. Now Ahmet was working in the kitchen with just one helper and there was just one servant who cleaned and served. "Don't worry," I said excitedly, "I am here and now we can cook together. You can teach me, and if I am good maybe you will give me all your secrets? I want to learn all the Egyptian dishes."

Ful Medames

This dish is traditionally cooked overnight and can be made with canned Egyptian small fava beans. Egyptian pickles are a mix of turnips, onions, and hot peppers and are available in Middle Eastern groceries. Cover 1 pound dried Egyptian fava beans with water and soak overnight. The next day, drain the beans and place in a large saucepan with 1 head of garlic, cut in half. Add 2¾ pints water and bring to the boil. Lower to a simmer, add 6 eggs in their shells, the juice of a lemon, and salt and pepper to taste. Cook the beans for 12 hours, or until tender, checking occasionally and adding water if needed. Prepare 6 individual bowls. Place 1 tablespoon chopped spring onion, 1 tablespoon olive oil, ½ tablespoon lemon juice, and salt and pepper into each bowl. Peel the eggs and place one in each bowl. Spoon in the ful *and serve with Egyptian pickles and toasted pita. Serves 6.*

Ahmet laughed, and the sparkle in his eyes returned. "You are so much like your grandmother. Egyptian recipes? All right . . . maybe we will cook a meal together for Vita's birthday next week." Vita was my favorite cousin. He had been away in Europe but was coming back to see his parents. The following Monday we went together to the market. Ahmet showed me how to choose eggplants for *babaghanou;* from there we went to buy quails for dinner. The quails were so much smaller than in Paris. I remembered how my grandfather and I had a little game of who would leave fewer bones on the plate after eating three quails. Returning to the house, Ahmet sent me away. "Let me prepare the birds and the vegetables," he said. "Then when I start cooking you can come back. Remember how your grandmother wanted you out of the kitchen? Well, she was right. You know, I miss her a lot, especially our daily arguments."

I left and went to read in the garden for half an hour and then silently crept back into the kitchen. Ahmet was plucking the quails and softly singing to himself. As I came in I said, "How will I learn how to pluck quails if you don't show me?" Ahmet laughed and handed me a tiny quail. "Pull the feathers in the opposite direction and cut off his feet." I tried and it seemed difficult at first but quickly I got the knack of it. While we were plucking the quails, Ahmet talked about his future. "I miss your grandmother so much." Ahmet sighed as he told me that money was tight but appearances had to be kept. "I cook what I want, but it is not the same without her. Next year I will go back to my village . . . but," and he smiled, "now that you are here we can talk about dinner together." We then marinated the quails in limes and olive oil; we broiled the eggplants and peeled the garlic. The smell of the kitchen was enchanting and made me dizzy with hunger. "I need something to eat. Will you make me a sandwich of *ful medamas*?" "Like old times," he said as he handed me a small pita filled with *ful* and pickles. I asked Ahmet about Ibrahim, his son. "He works at the hotel in town.

He is waiting for me to go back to our village in the Sudan. Your uncle promised him the job of guardian for the house. He hates to cook. He got married, you know? His wife is a good cook, but not like you," and he smiled affectionately at me. "I have to teach you how to make *sanbusaks* but I also want to teach you French recipes." I agreed to everything he said as long as he kept his promise to teach me all he knew.

It seemed to me that from the outside, the revolution and the new regime had not affected my family, but in reality it had. Business was bad, and the government was harassing the Europeans and the Jews. New regulations on import-export were piling up on my uncle Albert's desk, changing every day. When, after a few days, I tried to find out what was going on with my trial, my uncle told me that he was taking care of everything. It wasn't for a young woman like me to bother with these details. I was here to meet people, have fun, and hopefully get married. Now I understood why Clément had sent me back to Cairo. I was nineteen and had to get married or I would become an old maid! So I didn't ask about my uncle's legal appeal again. Instead, I was dragged to the Sporting Club each morning to go swimming and flirt with boys who happened to disapprove of bikinis, to my dismay. In the afternoon, my aunt took me shopping. According to her I needed lots of new dresses to go dancing in. My cousin Renée, who was my age and also unmarried, told me to be careful. "Don't go out alone with a man more than twice," she warned me. "If you do, they will announce your engagement. Try to go in a group or with me." Every Friday I was invited to dinner with one or another member of my family. There was always a young man there, and often he invited me out on the balcony to look at the stars, announcing that his future wife would get a large diamond and lots of servants to do her bidding. I was unimpressed.

I wanted to visit the Convent of the Sacred Heart, but I hesitated, not wanting to offend my family. I knew that they would not understand and worse, would feel betrayed by me. With the new regime, even though Jews had lived in this country for three hundred years, they were treated like foreigners. Unfortunately they looked European, their children did not speak Arabic fluently, and they all had gone to French lycées. Some of the preeminent families, foreseeing what was going to happen, had already left the country. My family felt strongly that they were Egyptians and should stay. Today there is no one left there.

Time in the kitchen with Ahmet was the best part of my day. I learned how to make *sanbusaks,* wonderful small pastries filled with cheese; *mulukhiyya,* the green herb soup; stuffed vegetables with rice and meat; and my favorite dessert, *loukomadis,* tiny fried balls of dough rolled in honey. My aunt, who prided herself on her European roots, adapted French recipes by using Egyptian spices. She taught me how to stuff a whole green cabbage with chopped lamb, herbs, and a dash of cumin, and to prepare a chicken basted with lime juice and garlic.

A month after my arrival, Renée and I decided that we should both find ourselves something to do besides shopping. My great-grandfather and my grandfather had founded orphanages for poor Jewish children, so we presented ourselves to the provost of one of these, asking for jobs. We were hired on the spot. Three times a week we left the house to go "shopping" and ended up at the orphanage, and nobody at home was the wiser. We brought the children, housed in a dreary, decrepit building, candies and cookies and taught them French songs and poetry. I felt that I was doing something worthwhile, but my uncle discovered our secret only three weeks later and called us into his office. "You cannot go back. You understand, Colette, people think we have lost our money. We can't let them believe that, so you can't work . . . no more teaching." I tried to argue that it was volunteer work, but Albert was intransigent. I went back to swimming, shopping, and parties in the evening. A week later, my uncle got a message from the city's chief of police asking for my hand in marriage. I laughed when I heard but my uncle said it was no laughing matter. The man had been at the airport when I was detained and had fallen for me. In his proposal he promised that he would take only one wife, and that I need not become a Muslim. My uncle said that we had to be very careful how we turned down his proposal. The entire family gathered in my uncle's apartment to discuss the matter. It was dangerous for all of us, my cousin Bernard said. We could be in real trouble, depending on how we responded. *I will never marry an Egyptian police chief,* I thought. *I will run back to Paris. After all, I'm French and they can't keep me here.* It was Tante Marie who came to the rescue. She suggested that we accept the marriage proposal, adding that my future husband should know that there was syphilis in the family. We waited impatiently for his answer, which came a week later. To the family's relief he withdrew his offer. For a few days I became the butt of family jokes. "When you go out, cover your face or if you don't the chief of police will catch you and . . ."

Renée and I tried to find something else to do. In Cairo there was a large Jewish hospital where I had had my appendix removed when I was young. I knew the surgeon, a friend of my father, so Renée and I asked him if we could work as volunteers, helping the nurses. This time Albert was supportive although he insisted that we be driven to the hospital every day instead of taking public transportation. Most of the Europeans had left the city, and the streets were filthy. Cairo's infrastructure was collapsing and had lost the pulse of a thriving metropolis. Luxury departments were poorly run and losing money. Houses were not repaired, and transportation like the trams were now in poor condition. Most of the expensive villas were abandoned by their owners. But I still found places I had once loved. On the way home from the hospital, I'd make the chauffeur stop in front of a *ful medamas* or falafel stand and buy a sandwich filled with the tasty beans or fried chickpeas, to Renée's horror. She'd cry, "Colette, you are going to get sick. These stores are so dirty!" I never did.

My assignment in the hospital was in the operating room. I loved watching the doctors as they cut. I wasn't squeamish; I'd come home at night wanting to tell everyone all the gory details while digging into Ahmet's fish wrapped in vine leaves and served with a tahini sauce. Two months later, because of an incident on the Israeli-Egyptian border, there was unrest in the street. The hospital, Jewish owned, was attacked by a mob, police were everywhere, and my uncle, fearing for our safety, forbade us to go there again. We were back once more to shopping and parties. I was secretly plotting to go back to Paris when fate took my side.

One night at dinner, I was seated next to a tall blond man of about thirty who did not seem Egyptian. During dinner I learned that his parents were Hungarians but that he had been born in Cairo. He had gone to school in France before the war and was an architect. He talked to me about an Egyptian architect called Hassan Fathi, who was using ancient Egyptian architectural forms in building modern houses. If I was interested, he would be happy to show me some of these buildings. This was the first time in months that I met someone who interested me, so for the next few days, I allowed Philip to take me around. I had never really looked at Cairo before. My world had always been the surroundings of Garden City with its luxury villas, the Convent of the Sacred Heart, Zamaleck, and the Sporting Club. Philip took me to the Dead City, in the heart of old Cairo, a village of four-hundred-year-old tombs and ancient dwellings with children running around half-naked. I visited for the first time old mosques and the pyramid of Saqqara, a magnificent stepped pyramid. The only ones I had seen were the famous three pyramids at Giza, which now had a gate around them and a musical extravaganza at night. I had a very good time with Philip, and at night I went dancing with him. We spent hours in the Egyptian Museum, where he recounted the stories of ancient Egyptian history. My family was ecstatic, and Tante Beca wrote my mother in Paris that finally, soon, she hoped, I would be engaged to be married. My mother, upon receiving this news, wrote to her best friend, Alice, in Boston that I was getting married. Alice ran an art store in Cambridge. Jimmy, who was then studying architecture at Harvard, happened to know her. The day my mother's letter arrived at the store, Jimmy came in to buy supplies, and Alice told him the great news. Jimmy, as he would tell me later, ran out of the store and sent me a telegram, which read: "Don't marry anyone but me. I love you." The telegram was like lightning hitting me. I hadn't heard from him in many months, and though I had not forgotten him, I thought that he had forsaken me. I showed the telegram to my aunt. "I am going back to Paris," I said. "I want to marry Jimmy. You must help me convince Uncle Albert." My aunt decided that the best way was to go and see a sheik, who was a well-known clairvoyant. She said he could tell the future. The next day we drove outside the city to a small village. We stopped in front of a stone house with open windows and an inner courtyard filled with goats and pigeons. A young barefoot Arab boy led us to a small room where a man in a long robe was sitting on the floor munching on roasted melon seeds. We sat on cushions, and while my aunt explained in Arabic why we were there, I stared at him. The man was old, with deep lines in his face and deep-set dark eyes that were looking at me. If I looked back at this man, right into his eyes, maybe I could convey to him my wishes. The sheik asked my aunt for a handkerchief that belonged to me. As he sniffed the handkerchief he said to my aunt not to keep me here any longer. I would end up far away on another continent with a tall dark-haired man. She would never see me again but I would be happy and it was the will of Allah that I go. It was written in the stars.

My aunt was astonished, and I was elated because now I knew that even if Jimmy did not come back for me (though I knew in my heart that he would), I would be able to return to Paris to study and to start my life. On the long way home my aunt said nothing, and we both rode in a silence heavy with our private thoughts. At dinner that night my aunt told Uncle Albert that he had to send me back. The trial with the government was going nowhere and I no longer needed to stay. I had a place to live and I could go back to the university. "She can have a job and work if the money disappears." The next few days were hectic. My aunt insisted that I have a trousseau, "just in case this tall young man comes." We bought towels with my initials, linen tablecloths, and sheets, which I still have today and which my daughters covet, to my surprise. I was given a big send-off party. My aunt surprised me with a new dress for that going-away party. The dress was beautiful, and that night I went to Tante Marie's room to show her my dress. "You look lovely; I will miss you," she said, and after spitting three times she suddenly, before I could do anything, cut off a piece of my dress. "No, no, don't do that," I cried out, but she said in a very firm voice, "Colette, it is to protect you from the evil eye. I want to be sure that you are going to be happy." Today, like Tante Marie, I make my children spit three times when news too good to be true arrives. For that party the food was incredible. All my aunts went to work with Ahmet. There were five types of dips, stuffed vines leaves served with yogurt, Ahmet's famous leek chicken, a galantine of duck, tiny roasted quails, and Tante Fortuné's best dish—a magnificent array of vegetables stuffed with rice and nuts, and redolent of cumin and garlic. There were five or six desserts, including one of my favorites, prunes cooked in tea and stuffed with walnuts, served with thick heavy cream. I said goodbye to all my friends and to Philip, who seemed unhappy to see me go. I knew I would never see them again. Renée was going to follow me to Paris a few months later. She also had not found a husband in Cairo. She would later marry an Englishman, have five children, and work hard to keep her family together. I never saw her again after that summer.

I would have to wait twenty years before I returned once again to Cairo. This time I went back with my daughter Juliette, who was writing an article on Egypt's millionaires. We stayed in a hotel in the middle of the Nile. As I looked out of the window at the traffic below, I realized how much Cairo had changed. There were skyscrapers, new highways, and the Nile was clean but there were no *felouk*, these beautiful ancient boats gliding on its surface that carried merchandise and people up the river. The boats were now moored in front of the hotels and used only to take tourists for a small ride back and forth. I went out that evening to look at my old house. I had a hard time finding it, as it had been sold to a rich Egyptian who had taken my grandfather's apartment and transformed it into a bank. The mango tree, however, was still there. I felt sad looking at that house where I had been so happy. But it was time to let go of all my memories, and leaving Garden City, I joined my daughter. In the next few days, I just took her around to my favorite haunts—the restaurant in the market where we used to eat roast squabs, a stand for a *ful medamas* sandwich, and my favorite falafel store. On our last day we ended at the Convent of the Sacred Heart. Time had not been gentle to the convent. The government had taken most of its land but the school was still the best in Cairo, and the chapel that I often imagined in my dreams was still there. So I placed a bouquet of roses on the altar as the brides had done for so many years and we left for New York.

9

The Wedding

It was early May when I returned to my minuscule, empty flat in Paris, and I was overjoyed. I walked endlessly through the Marché aux Puces, an enormous flea market with alleys hiding copper pots, old rugs, dusty jewelry, and clothes from another era. In 1953 times were still hard, and the flea market had great finds. I bought a dresser, two posters of American film stars, and a large vase. The large oak dresser dominated my room, but I couldn't return it, so I put the vase, full of magnificent tulips, on it. With the posters on the wall and the smell of coffee wafting up from an apartment below, it was home.

Food was a problem. *Chambres de bonnes,* usually on the top floor of a building, were rooms that were owned by the apartment dwellers below. The maid was supposed to eat in the kitchen of the tenant she worked for. Today, these *chambres de*

171

bonnes have been transformed into elegant studios. Having no kitchen, I had to eat out three times a day. Breakfast was no problem—*café au lait* and a *tartine* (a piece of baguette slathered with butter) was all I needed. I had my lunch at a small bistro, most of the time a prix fixe *steak pommes frites* and salad. Sometimes I took *le plat du jour* (daily special), which might be a *suprême de volaille en meunière* (strips of chicken sautéed in butter) or *boudin noir* (blood sausages) with steamed potatoes. Dinner was more of a problem. If no one had invited me to dinner, I stopped at a *charcuterie* (delicatessen) and bought ready-made dishes to eat sitting at my desk. Often it would only be a few slices of ham or headcheese with a vegetable salad. I was happy but lonely—I didn't have many friends. School was not going to start until the end of September, and I tried to occupy myself by reading all the new novelists that I knew I was going to study in my comparative literature program: Simone de Beauvoir, Marguerite Duras, Robbe-Grillet. I also read Shakespeare and Hemingway, who were all the rage in Paris.

My best friend, Claudine, had gotten married to an Orthodox Jew and was now very religious. She had already given birth to a baby girl, and sometimes we talked on the telephone. One day she asked me over for dinner on a Friday night. I arrived with a large bouquet of flowers, following my grandmother's constant admonition when I was younger. As soon as I rang the bell, Shimen, her husband, opened the door and said rather gruffly, "Shabbat! We don't ring the bell . . . and leave the flowers outside; you don't carry anything on Shabbat." I was embarrassed but came in leaving my offering on the landing. Claudine was there, looking quite happy. A head scarf was covering her hair and she wore no makeup. There was another couple standing in the living room and a young man with a black beard. I played with the baby until we were all called to the table, which was covered with a transparent plastic tablecloth. A large silver candlestick had been placed in the center. Shimen prayed as the men bowed their covered heads before we started to eat. The evening was pleasant. Henry, the bearded young man (who had, of course, been invited to meet me), talked about his work as a scientist in an atomic laboratory in Paris where Shimen was his boss. As dinner ended, Claudine started to remove the dishes from the table. I got up to help, and thinking that the plastic tablecloth had to be removed, I lifted the candlestick, stopping in midair as everyone cried out, "Don't touch . . . it's Shabbat!" Again I felt embarrassed and realized that I was ignorant of Jewish religious customs. In my arrogant naïveté I thought, *I don't want to change . . . I don't want to become a religious Jew like her.* Instead of learning what Judaism was all about, I fiercely held on to my Catholic identity. That night I left Claudine's house feeling miserable, and thinking that I'd lost a friend forever. The next time I saw her was six years later, when I returned to Paris from New York. I had by then come to terms with being half Jewish and half Catholic, and I managed to rekindle my friendship with Claudine, which is still strong as I write this.

My cousins helped to combat encroaching loneliness during that year. My grandfather had had eight children and each was a parent. After the Egyptian revolution, some had gone to South America, others to Italy, Switzerland, and France. The great majority had chosen Paris because often their children had studied there and also they all spoke French and thought it would be easier to reestablish themselves. My favorite cousins were in Paris, all men except for Nadia, who had been brought up in South America. Nadia was about five years older than I, pretty, vivacious, and artistic. She was a very good painter, but was also interested in moviemaking and was thinking of becoming a producer. In Clément's eyes, Nadia was unconventional, and she shocked him by going to live with Hank, a young American who was enamored of French life and literature. From the first day we met, Nadia and I became great friends. I admired her and even envied the ease with which she spurned conventions and the older members of the family, whom she quickly alienated. I often escaped to her apartment and complained to her about my life. She said, "Leave . . . what are you afraid of?" But I was not ready to make a move. A year later, just before I left for Cairo, Nadia and Hank got married and went to Rome. I was sad to see her go, not knowing what an important role this move would play in my life.

Nadia had four half brothers. One, Samuel, was a hairdresser in Paris, whom I saw rarely, and one had stayed in Egypt, where he ran a perfume factory. Robert, the youngest brother, was studying medicine in Paris. Then there was Jean, who had married young. By the time I had moved into my little studio, he was only twenty-four and had already separated from his wife. A poet and writer, he took it upon himself to take care of me. Pierre, another cousin, a terribly pompous doctor, did not participate in our games and weekend outings. Nor did Paul and his wife, Doris, who had two young children and were quite successful. We all met at Clément's house about once a month. The rest of the time I spent going out with Jean, Robert, Nadia, and Hank. Clément was pleased that I spent weekends in the countryside with them, not suspecting that my two cousins and their friends were in love with me, especially Jean. They all kissed me tenderly and wrote me poems and long letters asking me to marry them. Although I enjoyed all the attention, I still remained the convent girl. I realized later that this was probably what attracted them to me.

In early May I received a letter from Nadia. She and her husband were involved in the presentation of Italian films at the Cannes Film Festival. Nadia had just given birth to a baby girl and needed someone to take care of her. Would I come? I jumped at the idea of spending two weeks in Rome. Clément agreed that it would be a good idea, and a few days later I took the train for Rome. As I entered the compartment that was assigned to me, I found it occupied by an Italian family—a father, a mother, and two small children spread out over all eight seats. I explained that one of the seats was mine, and after much commotion and discussion, the mother motioned me to sit in the seat beside her. Within an hour, she had practically adopted me.

* * *

When I was born, my mother had refused to breast-feed me on the grounds that I was a hungry baby and needed to be fed much too often. So, following the tradition of my Egyptian family, a wet nurse was summoned to the rescue. Maria, my wet nurse, came from the Abruzzi Mountains of Italy. She had had a baby six months earlier, and because she was poor, had decided to answer my mother's ad. Maria did not speak a word of French, so within a month the entire household picked up enough Italian to communicate with her. My first words were in Italian, and by the time I was five I spoke Italian almost as well as my native French. When we left for Egypt, Maria went back to her family. I had not spoken Italian for more than thirteen years. As soon as the train started to move, Angelica, my new Italian *mama,* brought down an enormous basket from the rack above our heads. From it she took out a tablecloth, which her husband, Luigi, spread on the folding table near the window. Then out came several plates, a large salami, marinated red peppers, a slab of fresh Parmesan, country bread, and a bottle of red wine. The smell of the salami invaded the compartment; I felt famished and hoped that Angelica would offer me something to eat. I looked the other way while Angelica served her children and husband. Then, turning to me, she offered me some food in broken French. I was ready to refuse politely, but found myself saying, *"Si, grazie!"* with fervor. Angelica explained that the garlicky salami was from Sardinia, and that she had prepared the peppers herself by cooking them very slowly in balsamic vinegar. I drank several glasses of wine. Halfway through the trip, slightly tipsy, I started to speak Italian as fast as they did. I played games with the children, drank espresso out of a Thermos bottle, and finally, around midnight, fell asleep, my head resting on Angelica's shoulder. The next morning, an hour before arriving in Rome, Angelica once more brought down the large basket and out came small pastries and a second Thermos bottle full of hot coffee. We exchanged telephone numbers, and Angelica promised that she would call me and invite me to her house for dinner. She never did, but I kept my memory of her alive by passing on her red pepper recipe to my eldest daughter, who has made it one of her signature dishes.

Nadia was waiting for me on the platform, waving her arms wildly when she saw me. She grabbed my arm with one hand and my suitcase with the other and said breathlessly, "Quick, let's go! We only have three days and I want to introduce you to all my friends before we leave!" While I tried desperately to get a glimpse of the city from the taxi window, Nadia chattered away about her friends, her *balia* (wet nurse)—who came from Abruzzi, just like Maria—and her new life as a mother. She stopped talking only when we reached her house. Nadia lived in a lovely apartment near the Tiber River. Hank, so undeniably American, albeit charming, spoke bad French and bad Italian, wore a bow tie and khaki pants, and carried his glasses perched on the end of his prominent, ruddy nose. He was the Italian correspondent for the American movie trade magazine *Variety* and loved living in Rome.

Baby Amy was only six months old and adorable. Lucia, the wet nurse, was not very happy to see me, I soon discovered; she had hoped to find herself alone with Amy and to have her family move in while Nadia was away. With me there that was impossible. That night we sat down to my first full Italian meal. We started with paper-thin slices of prosciutto served with fresh mozzarella. This was followed by an incredible dish of fresh pasta with a pesto sauce and freshly grated Parmesan. Tiny wild strawberries marinated in white wine ended the dinner. I was enthralled by the food and the view of the Tiber from the terrace.

The next day Nadia and I went around town so she could introduce me to her friends. We started with an old journalist. "A powerful woman," Nadia whispered as we entered her house, "but be careful . . . she's an infamous lesbian and loves young girls. If she likes you, she will invite you to her parties but don't go to her house during the day." Signora Laeticia, as everyone called her, was a woman in her late fifties—ugly dyed-red hair, thick glasses hiding beady eyes. She was beautifully dressed, with a jeweled cigarette holder at the corner of her very red lips. "Ah . . . this is your lovely cousin? Well, we'll have to take care of her, won't we?" and turning toward me, she added in her slippery voice, "Join us next Saturday, *carina*. I am having a large dinner party and you can meet all my friends." When we left the Signora, Nadia was beaming like a mother hen who had just won first prize for her chick. The next few hours were devoted to making the rounds of the young painters on the rise who were Nadia's friends. The first one was Hugo Attardi, an artist then in his thirties, who is today one of Italy's most famous sculptors and painters. I liked him immediately, and when he invited me to the beach for the following week, I said yes without hesitation. From there we went to see Renato Guttiuso, a Sicilian painter about Nadia's age, with a ruddy face and a two-day-old beard. I was famished, but Nadia did not seem to want to stop anywhere to eat. Luckily, at Renato's studio we were offered wine and *bruschetta,* thick slices of country bread, brushed with olive oil and smothered with chopped tomatoes and basil. I ate and drank wine with such eagerness that Renato laughed. He turned to Nadia and said, "I like the girl. Don't worry . . . we will all take care of her." Our last stop was to the Via Margutta, near the popular Piazza del Populo, to visit Nadia's best friend, Giuliana, a journalist who had left her husband and lived with another journalist also named Renato. She was on dangerous ground, since in Italy at the time, divorce was not legal and living in sin in the eyes of the church could jeopardize Giuliana's financial arrangement with her husband. I was drawn to her and her boldness. Her apartment was crowded with books, papers strewn everywhere, contemporary paintings on every wall. Like Nadia's other friends, Giuliana promised that she would keep an eye on me and have me over. That night, over a buttery risotto with artichokes, Nadia gave me her last instructions. "Don't go to bed with everyone (as if I—the confirmed good Catholic girl—would), be sure that Amy is happy, don't let Lucia bully you, and call me once a week." I promised

I would follow her instructions, and the next day, after giving me a tour of the neighborhood, Nadia and Hank left for Cannes.

The first few days were exciting. I walked around Rome, stopped at cafés for espresso, ate *panini*, small brioche sandwiches filled with prosciutto or cheese for lunch, and went home in the evening to see Amy. Lucia cooked dinner. Every night we ate pasta with a different sauce. My favorite one was a rich, thick *ragu Bolognese* made with a mixture of veal and beef and fresh tomatoes, topped with freshly grated Parmesan. Lucia

Bolognese Sauce

Peel and slice 1 large carrot, trim 1 celery stalk, and peel and slice 1 medium-size onion. Place all the vegetables in a food processor and process until all the vegetables are minced. In a large saucepan heat 2 tablespoons olive oil and add 2 slices of bacon, cut into ½-inch pieces. Sauté until the bacon is crisp. Remove with a slotted spoon and discard. Add the vegetables and sauté over medium heat for about 5 minutes. Add 1½ pounds of chopped meat, half veal and half beef. Sauté for 2 minutes and add ¾ cup chicken stock, ⅔ cup white wine, and 2 tablespoons tomato paste. Mix well and correct the seasoning, adding 1 tablespoon oregano, ⅓ cup chopped basil, and salt and pepper to taste. Lower the heat and simmer for 45 minutes, adding more chicken stock if necessary. Serves 4.

always drank two or three beers with dinner. When I asked why, she answered proudly, "But Colette . . . it is very good for my milk and Amy will sleep well tonight." I followed suit when I was nursing (just one beer, though) and I've advised my daughters to do the same. They were not as willing as I.

The following Saturday both Hugo and the old journalist called, the former to remind me of his invitation to a day on the beach, the latter with an offer for lunch at her house. Remembering what Nadia had said, I politely declined the lunch invitation and agreed to go to the beach with Hugo and his friends. Hugo had a strong, rich baritone, and all the way to the beach, he sang old Italian love songs. As we lay on the beach I heard him murmur to his friends, "Don't touch! She's mine and I alone will look after her." I was flattered and wary at the same time. Hugo might have been sexy, but he was also married, Nadia had been sure to tell me. His wife lived near Naples for business reasons. Although I wanted, deep down, to have an affair with Hugo, it was unthinkable. That night as we drove back to Rome, we stopped at a small trattoria for a plate of fried calamari, a fennel salad, and lots of red wine. Hugo asked me to come home with him. Afraid to lose him as a friend and admirer, I replied, "Not tonight. I have to be home with Amy." As I got out of the car, I turned to him, bent down and kissed him lightly on the lips. "See you soon," I said in a quivering voice, hoping that I didn't sound too stupid. This scene was repeated for several days. I would bring up Amy's name, and Hugo, with an ever-deepening sigh, would drive away. At the end of the week Hugo asked if I would sit for him; he wanted to paint my portrait. And so for two weeks every day I sat on a chair, with an open blouse, half my breast showing. Hugo sang while painting or talked about his ambitions as a painter, about politics, and about love. I did not always understand; just listening to his voice seemed all that mattered. Friends dropped by in the late afternoon and I ran back to Amy, feeling guilty for abandoning her. A week later Hugo announced that he was leaving for two weeks and upon his return, he hoped Nadia would be back. I never saw him again.

I had been in Italy for three weeks, and still Nadia and Hank had not returned. Finally, they called. Hank wanted to meet and interview all the producers and actors who had congregated in Cannes. Did I mind? Of course I didn't mind. Another two weeks in Rome—what could be better?

A few days later Lucia came to me. She had not seen her child for over six months and asked if I would consider taking her back to her village. She could not go without me, as Nadia had made me responsible for Amy. I agreed to go, and on Saturday morning Amy, Lucia, and I took a train to her village. When we got off onto the platform, a band of four musicians started to play. No one else occupied the platform, so I understood that they were playing for us. Out of nowhere a woman of about forty ran up to me, smiling through her tears and saying over and over, "Colette, Colette!" I knew right away this was Maria, my old wet nurse. We embraced, and she introduced me to her son, who was my age, and her two younger daughters. We walked to the village, and to my astonishment, a very long table had been set right in the middle of the piazza. We sat down, the mayor made a toast, and enormous bowls of spaghetti with a rich tomato sauce were placed on the table. We ate, drank, ate again, and talked about the past while Lucia was showing off Amy and embracing her own children. Later, tired but happy, we took the train back to Rome. Suddenly, Lucia bent down, kissed me, and whispered, "Thank you."

The following week Nadia returned to Rome. I stayed another week but then Clément requested that I return to Paris and prepare myself to enter the Sorbonne. I left for Paris after saying goodbye to all my new friends, not knowing what was in

Red Peppers

Wash and wipe 6 large red sweet peppers. Cut each pepper in half and remove all the seeds and the white membrane. Then cut each half in two. In a large skillet heat ½ cup balsamic vinegar (it is important that you buy the cheaper balsamic vinegar as the aged one would be too strong). Add the peppers and 1 teaspoon coarse salt. Lower the heat, cover, and simmer for 45 minutes, stirring the peppers from time to time until they are tender and caramelized. Remove to a bowl and pour 2 tablespoons hot olive oil over them. When cool, refrigerate. Serve with salad and cold meat or fish. Serves 4.

store for me and hoping that one day I would come back. I returned to Rome thirty years later and went looking for Hugo, who was by then famous. I learned that my portrait hung in a museum in San Francisco as the *Woman of Tomorrow*. I met Hugo at his studio; he was now close to eighty and did not remember who I was.

A letter from Jimmy was on my little table when I returned home. He was graduating from Harvard, was going to be drafted into the army, and had asked to join the Counter Intelligence Corps. He was hoping that by the end of the year he would be able to come and see me. While waiting for the Sorbonne to start, I began to inquire about becoming a flight attendant (only back then, they were called hostesses), thinking that if he could not come to Paris, I would go to New York. It turned out I was too short (and most likely a little too plump), so I had to stay in Paris, study, and wait.

Autumn and winter passed rather uneventfully as I studied and spent weekends in the countryside. In early March, after a weekend with my cousins, I came back to find a message from my mother saying that Jimmy was in Paris looking for me and that she had given him my address. He would come by Sunday night and I should wait for him. I waited and waited. By eleven o'clock there still was no sign of Jimmy. So I undressed and, brokenhearted, went to bed. Half an hour later my buzzer rang and Jimmy was downstairs. I told him to come up, dressed in two minutes flat, and opened the door to see him smiling wearily and as handsome as I remembered him. His shy smile rekindled all my passion for him in seconds. He looked taller than I remembered, and travel worn. He sat on my bed and said in a low voice, "Colette, I hate the army . . . I am so miserable." I held his hand, kissed him, and suggested that we go out to a café and talk. We left Avenue Foche and walked toward the Etoile. It was late but the streets were still filled with people. I suggested that we walk down the Champs Elysées and find a restaurant where we could sit and talk. At that time it was lined with boutiques and cafés, not luxury stores and sports car showrooms as it is today. We ended up in a restaurant dear to me to this day, called Le Jour et La Nuit, open all night. We talked for hours, half in French (his was poor), half in English (my English had greatly improved). Instead of being stationed in France, which he had hoped, he had been sent to Munich, Germany. By four o'clock we returned to my studio. He reclined on my bed and I was wondering what I should do—the convent schoolgirl was battling with the Parisian sophisticate—when I looked down and saw that he was fast asleep. I lay down next to him and waited until morning for him to wake up. In my head I was already dreaming of how I would undress, how we'd make love, how he'd caress me. Almost as soon as he opened his eyes, he began to speak. It was a flood. "I love you. I want you to come to Munich and stay with me. I cannot live without you. To make love now is wrong. I have to leave in two hours to go back to Munich. It would be unfair. I will write and prepare everything for you there and you will join me. Promise me!" We kissed and hugged. I was disappointed but I promised I would come. We spent the next few hours walking in Paris just as we had done a few years earlier. We took the métro to Saint-Germain-des-Prés on the Left Bank and sat at the Café Flore. Sartre often held court there, surrounded by hopeful young writers listening attentively to his words. After spending an hour talking about our future, Jimmy, as always, said he was hungry. So we walked behind the church of Saint-Germain-des-Prés. Behind it was a large seafood market. Merchants were selling shrimps, cooked and uncooked, oysters, clams, and all sorts of fish. The street was bustling with housewives shopping for the weekend. I bought Jimmy some cooked *crevettes grises*, tiny little shrimps that he ate as we walked. The Left Bank was just starting to become the center of avant-garde fashion. Today the street is filled with boutiques of well-established fashion designers. Then, young designers were opening small stores in the Rue de Grenelle and the Rue des Saint-Pères. Later, as we strolled down Rue Jacob, we found old bookstores selling architectural books. Jimmy would have stayed there for hours but I was afraid he would miss his train. I took him to the station, kissed him over and over again, and cried without shame when the train left me in the middle of a crowd of commuters.

For the next two weeks I received daily letters. One had a curious drawing of a man cut into small squares, each square representing a day of his life in the army. Some were blackened—days gone by, he explained. Others were just white to represent the weekends "that didn't count." The remaining squares were gray, and there seemed to be many of them.

The following month Jimmy announced that he had obtained a week's leave and asked me to visit him. I went to see my mother and stepfather and announced that I was leaving for Munich. My mother started to cry, only because she was worried about what people would say, but my stepfather gave me his unequivocal blessing. With Clément I had to be more careful since he controlled the purse strings, so I lied. I told him that I had been offered a temporary job at the French Consulate in Munich and that the university had been apprised and would accept my work sent in from abroad. Clément bought it and I was off.

The train ride to Munich was interminable. I daydreamed all the way, trying to imagine what it would be like to be with Jimmy. I was scared . . . suppose it didn't work between us? Could my mother and Clément be right? Then I thought of Nadia. She was happy; it had worked for her, so why not for me?

Jimmy was waiting at the train station. Once I was wrapped in his long arms, I knew I had made the right decision. He had reserved a room in a hotel in Schwabing, where university students lived, and reassured me that no one there would ask questions. All I remember about that night was that we made love on what seemed like every surface in the room. . . . The next morning I woke up and looked at Jimmy sleeping next to me. I bent down and kissed him. I kissed him hard. He was my lover and I loved him more than anything in the world. As he opened his eyes and smiled at me, I felt at once tied to him and free as a bird.

Life was great and I wanted to make love again and again. For the next few days we drove through Munich in his small Morgan convertible, made love as often as we found the chance, and drank countless steins of beer in beer halls with Jimmy's college friend Les, whom I had met in Paris when I was sixteen. We ate sausages with sweet mustard on slices of brown rye bread, potato salad, and herring with onions. Munich still was suffering from the effects of the war, and bombed buildings were slowly being cleared and rebuilt. The city was occupied by the Americans, only Berlin was divided into four zones. The Russians occupied East Germany, and Jimmy explained to me that it was dangerous to cross the border but that sometimes young lonely Americans would slip away with their German girlfriends. After three days Jimmy sheepishly told me that he was running out of money and time—his leave was about to end.

We decided to rent a one-room flat in Schwabing. I wrote to Clément that the job had become permanent, told the truth to my stepfather and mother, and explained that my monthly allowance would pay the rent, and Jimmy's salary as an enlisted man would take care of the rest. Thus my daily life with Jimmy began.

In some ways it was not easy. At six in the morning Jimmy would leave for his office in the army barracks and not come back until the evening. I spoke not a word of German and couldn't find a job, not even giving private French lessons. After all, the Germans had lost the war, and learning French was not a priority. In the morning I shopped for food, learning idioms and phrases in German. I didn't know how to cook and had no cookbooks, but I remembered the trips I took with my stepfather, the restaurants we visited, and the guessing games we played about ingredients. So every day I chose a dish I had liked. I would make a list of the ingredients I thought were in the dish. I remember how I enjoyed choosing a vegetable or a piece of meat. Laden with my purchases, I trotted back to our tiny apartment, looking forward to preparing the dish or at least attempting to. Sometimes it took several attempts until I got it right. (I had nothing else to do.) I made cheese soufflés, roast duck with apples, coq au vin, and crêpes for dessert. Very soon I stopped trying to re-create the dishes I had eaten with my stepfather and started to cook my own recipes. I would walk through the market and see some vegetables I liked, buy them, then look for a chicken or a piece of pork, trying to imagine what the two would taste like together. As time went by I became more adventurous. Some nights I ended up with a disaster and everything went into the garbage and I'd go back to dishes I really knew. Other nights I received a telegram from Jimmy saying simply, *"Pas ce soir, Joséphine . . ."* (the famous message Napoléon used to send to Joséphine when he was at war). Jimmy's code meant that he was in East Germany trying to catch a young American soldier who had crossed illegally. Occasionally, Jimmy went away for several days on maneuvers with his unit. I hated these times because I had no friends in Munich. My German had not improved, and the officers' wives kept away from me, considering me a prostitute. I explored Munich, went to the movies, and read. Jimmy brought me books from the library. I read all the American classics, even a history of slavery in six volumes. My English improved and weekends were magical, spent exploring the countryside in Jimmy's Morgan.

Cheese Soufflé

First make a béchamel sauce: In a saucepan heat 1¼ cups milk over low heat to the boiling point. Remove from the heat. In another saucepan melt 2 tablespoons butter. When the butter is hot add 2 tablespoons flour all at once and mix well with a wooden spoon for 3 minutes. Then slowly add the milk, stirring all the while. Add salt and pepper to taste and simmer, stirring, for about 8 minutes. Remove from the heat. Butter an 8-cup soufflé dish. Sprinkle the bottom with 2 tablespoons grated Gruyère. In a bowl mix together 1¼ cups grated Gruyère with freshly ground pepper. Add 6 egg yolks, one by one, and mix well. Correct the seasoning with salt and pepper and a pinch of nutmeg. Add the Gruyère mixture to the béchamel and mix well. In a bowl beat 8 egg whites with a pinch of salt until stiff. Slowly add one-third of the whites to the yolk mixture, mix well, and fold in the remaining whites. Pour into the soufflé dish and bake in a preheated 375-degree oven for 45 minutes. Remove from the oven and serve immediately. Serves 4.

*   *   *

By November, I had been in Munich for seven months when I realized that Jimmy had only eight months left in the army. We talked about his plans, and he told me that once he had been discharged in the United States, he would come back for me. I wanted none of that! He had left me once already, and I had waited four years to see him again. I was very upset and started to cry. Jimmy looked surprised. Didn't I know he loved me forever? "I want to get married," I cried. "Now!" He smiled, and pulled out a stack of papers from his briefcase—they were permission forms for an officer's request to get married. I wrote to Clément and my mother that I was engaged, and in June, on Jimmy's two-week leave, we drove to Paris so I could introduce him to everyone in my family. We stayed in my mother's house, since Clément had taken back my little studio. Although my stepfather, Mira, did not speak a word of English and Jimmy's French was not the best, they managed to communicate and got along well. We talked about the wedding. We had to get married first in Germany (an army rule) and then in Paris, since the French would not recognize the German wedding. I surprised everyone, including Jimmy, by announcing that I wanted a Jewish ceremony. Jimmy, Jewish by blood, had rejected his heritage many years before. I wasn't sure why I insisted. Perhaps, deep down, I wanted to be accepted by my family. And I wanted to atone for having been a Catholic while Jews were killed in concentration camps. Or was it just that I always did the opposite of what everyone expected of me? Clément said we could be married in a Jewish temple by the Grand Rabbi of Paris, whom he knew. He would pay for it. My stepfather said he would pay for the reception; the date, September 27, was set. My mother said that I needed a dress for the civil ceremony in Munich and a wedding dress for the Paris wedding. The reception was going to be in a private room, at Prunier, a famous fish restaurant on the Avenue Victor Hugo. My mother wanted to go shopping with me; all of a sudden, she was getting very excited by my wedding. I refused her help, and all alone bought a beige suit with a lovely blue hat for Munich. Finding the wedding dress was harder than I thought. Finally, Mira came to my rescue (the date was fast approaching) and sent me to the French designer Maggie Roof. I found a pale blue dress with a matching bolero to cover my shoulders. The dressmaker offered to make the same one in white. I demurred, saying proudly, "I'm not a virgin . . . blue will be just fine!" She blushed, and I had her promise me not to describe the dress, which would be ready just before the wedding, to anyone in my family. The next day we left for London to meet Jimmy's English relatives. His mother's brothers had stayed in London, while she and her sisters had emigrated to the United States. Maury was the one I liked best. He was a Labor member of Parliament. He was very much interested in Egypt and had helped save two young Jewish youths in trouble with the police. He greeted me with open arms and gave us a party in the House of Commons. Neither Jimmy nor I wanted to stay long in England, since we couldn't sleep together out of wedlock. I had to stay with his mother Anne's younger brother, a shy man with a silent wife who could not cook, not even breakfast! We tried several times to sneak away but failed and so, to my relief, after a few days Jimmy announced that we had to go back to Munich, where we were both expected to return to work.

Upon our return to Munich, Jimmy learned that the day we got married he would lose his clearance and could no longer be a Counter Intelligence officer but would become an ordinary soldier. Jimmy was upset, but he had only a few months before being discharged. He hoped he would not have to leave Munich, which he liked very much. The civil ceremony took place in a small palace in Munich's English Gardens, with Les and his wife as our witnesses. Only Jimmy's sergeant had accepted our invitation; the others still frowned on our relationship. We stood in front of a judge who made us a long speech in German, which none of us understood. Afterward, we all traipsed to Les's house for a breakfast of German pancakes, caviar, and champagne. Three weeks later we left for Paris.

In Paris we found Anne, Jimmy's mother, staying with my mother. It was not a fortuitous mix. My mother, elegant as usual, had bought a light brown lace dress for the wedding. She showed it to my mother-in-law, along with her velvet hat with feathers. My mother-in-law admired both the hat and the dress and showed my mother hers. The dress was made of many layers of green tulle, like an exaggerated ballerina's costume. "No hat?" asked my mother, trying to suppress her dismay. I was immediately commanded to take my mother-in-law to my mother's milliner. We went together, and Anne asked me all the way why on earth she would need a hat. "It's the custom here," I explained. "You'll be the envy of your friends in New York." We chose a delicate hat with a veil and two feathers that fell gracefully to one side. The fact that she looked lovely did not prepare her for the price. "A hundred dollars for a hat! I've never paid that for anything to wear in my life!" I insisted she buy it, and for the next thirty years, she brought up that hat whenever we argued about money, or anything else, for that matter. The next dilemma concerned jewelry. Both my mother and Anne had a large collection, but Jimmy was rather poor at the time and couldn't afford an engagement ring. He had already designed the wedding band and Anne had it made in England. Because she paid for it and brought it to Paris with her, Anne felt strongly that my mother should give me one of her rings. My mother refused and for the next two days, accusations went flying back and forth until I put my foot down. I insisted that I hated rings in general, and that the only one I would wear was a wedding band. Since that day, Jimmy has given me a wedding band for each important anniversary.

Clément insisted that Jimmy come to his house for a "chat." I was asked to wait in the living room while they talked over aperitifs in Clément's private study. Later, Jimmy, who was quite shaken up, told me that Clément had warned him that I was a rich girl with a hole in my pocket. I was to inherit money when I turned twenty-one (a few months later), and Clément insisted that Jimmy "control" me and take care of the money.

But a year later, the Egyptian government nationalized every-thing, blocked my bank account, and took over whatever stocks and property my father had left me. I was left with nearly nothing. When Jimmy wants to tease me about money, he says with a kiss, "I married you on false pretenses. You cheated me of a fortune!"

The day of the wedding, I locked myself in my bedroom and told everyone to leave for the temple. I did not want anyone to see me before I got to the ceremony, except Clément who was going to ride with me and escort me down the aisle. As I came out of my room all dressed up and appeared in front of Clément, a look of horror crossed his face. "Blue? Are you mad? No one in our family gets married in blue! Why are you doing this?" "Don't I look beautiful? I'm not a virgin and I've been mar-ried for nearly three weeks, so I could not get married in white."

We rode to the temple in silence. As we marched down the aisle, I saw Jimmy standing under a *huppa,* the traditional Jewish canopy under which the bride and the groom stand. As I stood near Jimmy, I whispered, "Look at me! Do I look beautiful? Do you like my dress?" He smiled as he turned toward me and whis-pered back, "You look great but why on earth are we here? And behave yourself!" The Rabbi made a speech in French, but I wasn't listening. I was thinking of Cairo, of my grandparents, of the small chapel in the convent. Why in fact was I here? I had made a mistake with my dress, and my uncles and aunts would talk about me later and laugh. All of a sudden, the ceremony was over; we signed the book and were given a marriage certificate.

All my relatives and some of my friends were at the reception. My aunts were sitting together gossiping about Jimmy and probably about me too. Wonderful tiny hors d'oeuvres were passed around and champagne was flowing. Taitinger had been a friend of my stepfather, and gift cases of champagne had been sent to the reception as his wedding gift. I had also invited Francis, the young man my grandmother had tried to set me up with. He looked grim and unhappy, so I sailed up to him smiling and offered him a glass of champagne. He took one sip, walked brusquely up to Jimmy, who was standing nearby, threw the rest of the champagne in Jimmy's face, and left quickly. Everyone gasped and murmured but Jimmy laughed and said to me, "I would have done the same had he taken you away from me." I laughed, drank more champagne, and felt elated.

My stepfather had reserved a room for us at the Plaza Athénée Hôtel, and when the reception was over we were driven there. As we were about to go to bed the telephone rang. It was Jimmy's friend; he was downstairs in the bar with all the young people from the wedding. "Come down! It's too early to go to bed. Come and celebrate with us." We were up until dawn. Forty years later, I wrote to the Plaza Athénée, asking for the same room we had enjoyed on our wedding night. Not only did we get the same room, we were charged the 1955 price! That night the Plaza invited us to their restaurant. The chef to whom I had written about what I had liked in 1955 organized the menu. We started with baked truffles. As we opened the foil packets and inhaled their aroma, memories of my first truffle with my stepfather flew into my head. I had loved that first truffle so much, and now after the first bite the same wonderful exciting feeling that here I was eating something so special came back to me. This dish was followed by tender filets of sole with almond butter; followed by a small sorbet of pear with eau-de-vie, then a tender, pink rack of baby lamb, next a salad, and finally, the most wonderful hot chocolate cake topped with the year 1955 made of spun sugar. We drank several bottles of wine. Drunk and happy, we went back to our room and that night, no one woke us up.

Before leaving for Austria on our honeymoon, we had breakfast with Mira and our two mothers. Mira took me to his room and told me that our wedding present from him was a gastronomic tour of France. He would organize it for the following June when Jimmy was out of the army. It would prove one of our most memorable trips together. Everything was arranged according to Mira's strict criteria. Two stars for lunch and three stars for dinner. Our first stop was Chartres. Once we had explored and marveled at its magnificent cathedral, we made our way to a restaurant in Belleme called Auberge des 3 J. We sat down to eat at one o'clock and left our table at four, having feasted on *persillé* of foie gras with mushrooms and an exquisite "poularde" stuffed with Camembert. The meal ended with a thin slice of *pain d'épices* served with crème fraîche and locally produced honey.

Within a couple of days, I could no longer eat two meals a day, but Jimmy continued to feast with gusto. The last restaurant we visited was Chez Point in Vienne. Mira had a close relationship with Point and had ordered the dishes well in advance. For three hours we savored the most exquisite meal of our lives and drank a huge quantity of wine. By the time we left the restaurant, my husband could barely walk. As we drove away, I quickly realized that he was drunk and that we had to stop at the first inn we saw. After ten minutes of terror on the road, I spied a small billboard advertising a hotel nearby. When we arrived (Jimmy stayed in the car, unable to move); the manager claimed that he had no vacancies. Panic crept into my voice as I pleaded with him. I explained that I was on my honeymoon, that my husband was drunk, that I wanted to live, and that I was certain he didn't want my death on his conscience. The man relented and showed us a room with a huge double bed and a mirror on the ceiling. We collapsed on the bed and fell asleep.

When I woke up during the night needing to find the bathroom, I went to the door and realized that we were locked in. We could not get out of the room! I tried to wake up my husband but failed to do so. I went back to bed thinking the manager was kidnapping us for ransom. I tried not to fall asleep, to stay alert, but when I was awakened by sunlight filtering through the wooden blind, I knew it was morning and that I had slept through the rest of the night. I ran to the door and to my relief I found it unlocked. As we paid for the room, I refrained from asking the manager why he had locked us in. I thought perhaps I had been dreaming. Later when I told my stepfather about the incident, he burst out laughing, "You ended up in the best whorehouse outside of Lyon!" he explained "He saw a young married couple and he did not want you to know what was happening in his 'hotel.'" He hugged me heartily, still laughing.

Mira had a second gift for me that long-ago day. After explaining the grand tour he had planned, he bent down and retrieved a box from under the hotel bed. He opened it and, to my astonishment, it was filled with gold coins. He chose a twenty-dollar gold coin and handed it to me. "You are going to America. I want you to have this," he said. I kissed him, thinking how good he was to me. Then Jimmy and I hopped into our little magenta sports car and sped off to Vienna and our new life together.

10

A Wife No Matter How You Say It

After our honeymoon, we went back to Munich. No longer "living in sin," I was now acceptable to all the army wives except for the fact that I had no children and each of them had several. I soon realized that we had nothing in common to talk about (I certainly wasn't interested in diapers and hairdos), and I stopped accepting their invitations. Most of the time I stayed home, cooked, and explored German markets. Munich was slowly beginning to revive itself, and rich Bavarian food was appearing in restaurants and shops. What I found astonishing was the number of sweet pastries and gobs of heavy cream Bavarians could eat. In the late afternoon, I'd go to a coffeehouse in my neighborhood for a rich, fragrant German coffee. I'd sit staring at women, sporting dark green or brown hats with small veils, devouring bowls of whipped cream, layer cakes slathered with chocolate and custard, and buttery pastries with jam. In delicatessens, I discovered smoked hams, headcheese with pickles, bologna, and liverwurst, which I enjoyed spreading on the moist brown bread for lunch. The meals I prepared in the evening were completely French, however. I sautéed pork chops stuffed with garlic and herbs and served them with a purée of parsnips; I braised a chicken with wild, fresh mushrooms and accompanied it with string beans tossed with garlic and parsley. The only dish that was influenced by Munich was *choucroute,* a dish based on sauerkraut cooked with sausages and smoked pork. I had to rinse the overly briny German sauerkraut and cook it slowly in white wine; only then was the dish mellow and refined.

Jimmy and I talked every night about our future and what we should do. The most pressing question was where we should go after Jimmy was discharged from the army. Paris? New York? Another city? As is often the case, fate made the choice for us. Jimmy found out that he was going to be kicked out of his unit for marrying a foreigner, a potential enemy in the eyes of the army, and be sent to Augsburg, a smaller city nearby where other American units were stationed. But the transfer papers moved very slowly, and in November we were still in Munich. Jimmy was entitled to a week's leave, so we decided to take a trip to Italy. While studying at Harvard, Jimmy had befriended a young Italian architect, Pietro, with whom he had spent all his free time. Upon graduation, Pietro suggested that Jimmy join him in Italy and become his partner in an architectural venture. Jimmy suggested we visit him in his hometown, Udine, in the north. I was happy to be back in Italy and proud that I had not forgotten my Italian. We were greeted warmly by Pietro and given the grand tour of his provincial but charming little town. We ate broiled chicken and fresh pasta and downed bottles of Tokai, the local wine in a trattoria called La Vedova (The Widow). In Italy we were poorer, and going to a restaurant meant eating most of the time at small, informal trattorias. We were regulars at the Vedova, with its open kitchen in the middle of the dining room.

Chicken Vedova

In Udine the chicken were free-range, small and scrawny. To make this dish you need poussins, or very small chickens. Cut four 1½- pound chickens in two. Rub the chicken with garlic cloves and then with 2 tablespoons lime juice. Sprinkle the chickens with salt and pepper. Mix 2 tablespoons oregano with 2 table- spoons thyme. Rub the chicken with the herbs and refrigerate for at least 1 hour. Just before broiling, rub the chickens with 2 tablespoons olive oil. Broil the chickens on one side for 8 minutes, turn them, and broil them for another 8 minutes. The broiling time depends on how large the chickens are. Serve the chickens with a salad of watercress. Serves 4 to 8.

Small, tender chickens were broiled on a charcoal grill in the center of the room. As guests sat wherever they wished, they were brought a pitcher of local wine, along with olives, sliced salami, and a basket of country bread. I loved that trattoria and felt more at home there than in a French bistro. Pietro again asked Jimmy to join him in his architectural studio. Pietro's father had been Udine's most respected architect, and now his son had taken over his father's practice with his sisters, who were also architects. I thought that it was a wonderful idea but wondered how we would live there. "I will take care of everything," Pietro insisted. "I will find an apartment for you and Colette, and you will get paid right away. Don't worry about anything." Jimmy accepted.

Upon our return, Jimmy announced to his commander that he wanted to be discharged in Munich. Within a few weeks his discharge papers were approved, and just before he was to leave his unit, they decided to give us a farewell party. This was my first encounter with a formal American dinner, which I have never forgotten.

The wives stood chatting in one corner of the living room while the men occupied another, and everyone was drinking hard liquor and smoking. I was shy among the women and contributed little to their chatter. I tried to listen in on the men's conversation, which centered on West Germany's attempt at becoming independent. I had a problem with America's political stance and its friendliness toward the Germans. After all, the Germans had lost but they were recuperating much faster than the French, a situation I resented. Also I had had an unpleasant incident a few days before. We had been to Octoberfest, a festival celebrating the newly made winter beer held in a large brewery's garden just outside Munich. Long tables were set up, and waitresses dressed in Bavarian costumes served large steins of strong dark beer. We were welcomed by the other guests as we sat down at one of the communal tables. They smiled, nodded and murmured, "American? Nice . . . have a beer on us." Jimmy smiled back and explained that he was American and I was French. The smiles disappeared immediately, and the free beer never materialized. I was shaken. Once I shook myself out of this reverie, I slowly drifted toward the men to listen further. I looked back at the women and realized immediately that I had made a mistake. They seemed upset so I worked myself back into the female fold. Later, we all sat down to dinner. The first course was boiled shrimps with a strange, slightly sweet red sauce that Jimmy told me later was ketchup. I hated it then and I still hate it. My children jokingly say they were deprived youngsters because I never allowed ketchup in the house. Next to the shrimps was a salad that I had never seen before. "What is it?" I asked one of the guests. "You don't know? Poor thing! You should come and shop with us at the commissary. This comes directly from home; it's iceberg lettuce." They were also sure I would love the thick pink sauce called French dressing poured on top of the salad. The lettuce was crunchy, cold, and had absolutely no flavor, and the pink dressing was nothing like the vinaigrette I was used to. I was confused as to why this food was not appealing, but I tried to eat a little anyway.

I also had a problem with the main course—roast turkey served with a red sweet jelly (all the sauces seemed to be a different shade of red!) and stuffed with a slightly doughy, overcooked mixture of breadcrumbs, celery, and onions. When I was asked what I would like to drink, I replied, "Red wine would be fine, thank you." There was muted laughter, and I was offered Coca-Cola instead. As a student in Paris, I had tried Coca-Cola and disliked its sweet medicinal taste, so the idea of drinking Coca-Cola with my meal seemed quite ridiculous to me. I asked for plain water and continued picking at my meal. The only thing that saved the day was dessert, a scrumptious American apple pie, plump, juicy, and infused with cinnamon. Later that evening the men played poker and I sat next to Jimmy, refusing to join the ladies in the other room. Later I thanked my hostess for a delicious meal. She said she would be happy to write down all the recipes. I thanked her again and explained that I wasn't much of a cook. A few days later, we packed and left in our little magenta sports car for a leisurely trip down to Udine.

Although Udine—the commercial and banking center of the Friulli-Venezia region of Italy—is a short car ride from Venice, they are completely different cities in every way. Whereas Venice is a gem of architecture, Udine has no famous monuments, no good restaurants, and especially no tourists. In the center of the town is a hill, which, legend has it, was built by Attila the Hun in order to admire from a distance the burning of Aquileia, a city that he had conquered. Everyone in Udine was very proud of this man-made hill; I, too, was enamored of it and often climbed to its peak to admire the magnificent valleys that surrounded the town.

Pietro put us up for the first few days in a small *pensione*, the Italian version of a bed-and-breakfast. Later that afternoon he took us to the apartment he had rented for us, which was in a very old building overlooking the market square, near Via Mercatovecchio, a busy street lined with small shops. The apartment was quite large with two bedrooms, a very primitive bathroom, no heat, and a bare kitchen with just two burners and a stone sink. With no furniture, no light, and a pervasive smell of decay, the apartment filled me with dismay. Jimmy did not seem to care, too excited by Udine, Pietro's studio, and the architectural work. We had very little money, since the Egyptian government sent us only about two hundred dollars a month while my suit with them was pending. That night in the hotel, I tried to discuss with Jimmy what we should do. Buy furniture? No, that was ridiculous. How would we get it back to the United States later on? Also, I pointed out to him, the apartment was too cold, and despite the fact that everyone in Udine looked at the blue sky and the bright sun and told me how warm the weather was, I was freezing. It was late October and it would soon get even colder. Jimmy suggested that I look around for another apartment. The next morning, armed with the local paper, I went searching for a real estate agent. I found Manuelo, newly in business and eager to practice his English. "I have to improve my English," he said. "If you help me improve, I will charge you very little because now that the American army has important headquarters here in Udine, its officers needed some help with apartments." "For the officers?" I asked. *"Ma no, signora,* for the girlfriends!" So sitting behind Manuelo on his little Vespa, holding on to his waist for my life, I went hunting for an apartment. Jimmy and I could not compete financially with the American officers, so we ended up on the edge of town, near the Italian barracks housing the Italian soldiers. Manuelo introduced me to his friend Signora Baldini, who, as a widow, had inherited enough money to build herself a villa. The attic was for rent and she offered it to me. The space was grand but it had no kitchen, no bathroom, and no heat. "How can we live here?" I asked Manuelo. Well, it turned out that Manuelo, knowing that Jimmy was an architect, had suggested to the Signora that Jimmy could design a bathroom and a kitchen and the Signora would build them and charge a reduced rent. Pietro thought it was mad, Jimmy loved the idea, and I was pleased. Within a month we moved in. The room was very large. Jimmy had designed a box in the center of the room, which housed the bathroom and divided the room in two. The bathroom had a bathtub, a sink, and a toilet. In a corner was a very primitive type of water heater. In order to have hot water, I would sit on the toilet and feed the hot-water heater with wood while Jimmy washed himself. Then he would do the same for me. On very cold days, I simply refused to wash.

On one side of the bathroom was the living-dining room, heated by a *stuffa,* similar to a Franklin stove, made of bricks but terribly inefficient. Jimmy drew several sketches of me literally sitting on the *stuffa* trying to warm myself. The kitchen was another problem. It was in the corner of the living room and consisted of a table with a two-burner portable range and the smallest refrigerator I had ever seen. Next to it was a stone sink with only cold water. How was I to cook? "Very easy," Manuelo said. "When you need to use the oven, go to the baker. He will bake for you!" Pietro lent us a bed, four chairs, a dresser, a round dining table, and an old couch. I went to the market to buy pots and pans, china and cutlery, and we were set to live in luxury, Italian style, for the next few years.

I bought myself a bicycle, and every morning after Jimmy left for the studio, I went shopping in the neighborhood. I was known as the American lady because at the butcher I insisted that my steaks be cut thick, not by an electric slicer. I learned how to distinguish good veal, make a real Bolognese sauce, and cook fresh pasta perfectly. In the evening we often went out to dinner with Pietro or with his sisters. La Vedova was our usual choice as was the house specialty—broiled chicken. I tried to get the recipe but the owner always refused. She finally gave in when I went to say goodbye before we left Udine for the United States. She handed me the recipe with a warm embrace.

The best part of my week was Saturday, market day. Merchants and farmers from around Udine came there to sell their fruits and vegetables, cooking utensils, dresses, and linens.

The market was packed. I had my favorite stands, like the one belonging to an old woman who sold shiny radicchio salad, artichokes, and bitter *rapini*. As soon as I got to the market she would call after me, "*Bambina, vieni qui.*" One day, I told her I was a new bride, and she insisted I buy a live turtle. "Good for marriage," she said. "Put her under the *stuffa*, feed her some lettuce leaves, and everything will be all right with you and your husband and you will have lots of bambini." I bought the turtle and took her home in a cardboard box. Once home, I placed the box under the *stuffa* as I had been instructed. Sometimes I took her out and let her roam the room. I would stroke her neck and feel as if she were some kind of goddess who was here to protect Jimmy and me. I loved her.

I often asked the old woman how to cook the seasonal vegetables she sold, and she gave me wonderful recipes—stewed eggplant with red peppers, and stuffed zucchini. The fruit stands were loaded down with magnificent melons, grapes, and tiny tangerines that perfumed the whole house. There was Hugo, who called me *la Francesa*. He sold small potatoes, thin string beans, eggplants of different shapes and colors, delicate baby spinach, and crunchy fresh fennel. Next to him was a glassed-in truck where I bought *porchetta*, the roasted pork roll stuffed with herbs, and salamis and prosciutto, from both San Daniele and Parma. In the spring the tomatoes, deep red and intensely flavored, made a superb tomato salad with red onions and fresh basil. The Saturday butcher was quite different from the one I went to during the week. He sold plump chickens that I would roast in the baker's oven and serve with spicy salt; small quails that could be pan-roasted; rabbit; pheasants; and very expensive veal. Manuelo introduced me to Signor Francesco, the olive oil merchant on Via Mercatovecchio. His dark shop was filled with enormous green glass bottles of olive oil wrapped in straw. The oils ranged from pale yellow to rich green, and Francesco invited me to taste as many as I wished, dipping pieces of bread into little crocks. He filled my bottles with a light-colored oil for cooking, a dark, more pungent one to drizzle over vegetables, and a fragrant, spicy one for salads. Next door, a similar shop was filled with wooden barrels of Tokai, and I'd buy several bottles that were delivered right to my door. Again, before I bought, I had to taste the different vintages. By the end of the morning, I was often slightly tipsy but always very happy.

The first week of November—we had been in Udine for a month—my landlady asked me for the rent. When I asked Jimmy for money, I found out we had very little left. Money hadn't yet arrived from Egypt, and Pietro's office had no money to pay Jimmy for his work. I decided that I should sell something before I wrote Paris for help. I still had twelve gold bangles that my grandfather had given me, as well as several gold coins. In the morning I went to the café on Piazza Libertà where I often stopped for espresso and where I gave the owner's daughter weekly English lessons so she could converse with her boyfriend, an American officer. Paola was hoping that he would marry her and take her to America. I sat down with her and explained my problem. She spoke to her father, and over the next three months, I sold three of my gold bangles, which paid the rent and for some of our daily expenses. I still struggled with our cold apartment. I would leave in the morning and roam the streets of Udine, trying to find stores that were well heated, buying nothing but keeping warm. Once again, Manuelo saved me. He told me that his American officers were looking for someone who spoke both English and Italian to teach them Italian. I went to meet the head of the unit stationed in Udine and was hired to teach Italian four times a week for two hours. My salary for postwar Udine was enormous—two hundred American dollars a month that Paola gladly changed into lire for me. "It's for my trip to America," she'd say. What pleased me even more than the cash was the warmth of the room where I taught. I always came an hour earlier and sat on the radiator, warming myself. Most of the time, the officers just wanted me to advise them about their girlfriends—what tender words to say and how to seduce them. Over the following months, we were secure. But as Thanksgiving approached, Jimmy began to be homesick. He missed his family, New York, and the food. He asked me if I would make a Thanksgiving dinner for the office and our friends. Thanksgiving? Jimmy explained the holiday and what was served: roast turkey stuffed with chestnuts, cranberries, Brussels sprouts, sweet potatoes, and pumpkin pie. I could find Brussels sprouts, but cranberries and sweet potatoes didn't exist in Italy. I would have to roast the turkey at the bakery. We

Roast Turkey

In a bowl mix together 1 tablespoon salt, 1 tablespoon pepper, 2 shallots and 2 onions, finely chopped, 2 garlic cloves, finely chopped, 2 tablespoons chopped parsley, 3 tablespoons red vinegar, 1½ cups white Vermouth or white wine, ½ tablespoon cumin, and ½ cup dark soy sauce. Rub this mixture on a 12-pound turkey and refrigerate overnight, turning the turkey twice. Meanwhile prepare the stuffing. In a bowl put about 25 dried apricots, soaked in brandy for 1 hour. Peel 3 green apples, cube them, and add to the bowl. Then add 3 cups peeled canned chestnuts, the grated rind of a lemon, salt and pepper to taste, and 1 table-spoon tarragon. Mix well and add 2 cups toasted bread cubes. Mix well. Remove the turkey from the refrigerator. Separate the skin of the breast and slide 1 tablespoon butter under the skin. Add 1 cup chicken stock to the stuffing and mix well. Fill the turkey cavity with the stuffing. Close the opening with foil. Place the turkey with the marinade in a roasting pan. Roast in a preheated 375-degree oven for 20 minutes per pound, basting very often with the marinade and ¼ cup melted butter. Remove the turkey from the oven and allow it to rest for 15 minutes before carving. Serves 8 to 10.

haggled over the price and he agreed to use his oven. Now, I had to find the turkey. On Saturday I went to the market and found a young boy who had poultry in wooden cages. I asked him if he had any turkeys. He did, and proceeded to hand me a beautiful live turkey; he was grinning, with a slightly mocking glint in his eye. No, I insisted, I'm not going to kill it myself! So after begging the boy for half an hour, I finally persuaded him to kill the turkey for a fee if I helped. We went to a dark alley around the corner, equipped with a large butcher's knife. I closed my eyes and trembled, holding the writhing turkey. I heard a swish, let go of the bird, opened my eyes, and saw a headless turkey running in circles. We finally caught it, and I bicycled home with the warm, dead turkey in my basket. The next day, I prepared the turkey, stuffed it, and took it to the baker's, telling him how long I wanted it cooked. I went down to Signora Baldini and baked a pumpkin pie (the French way), prepared the Brussels sprouts, and made a salad. After setting the table I went with Jimmy to get the turkey. It came out of the oven golden brown, filling the bakery with a wonderful smell of herbs and wine. Neighborhood kids, fascinated by the huge roasted bird, began to follow us down the street; it was like a scene from the Pied Piper. I promised the kids that if there was any turkey left I would bring it back to the baker for them. The dinner was a success, the leftovers were taken back to the baker's, and from then on I was known as "the nice American lady"; when we went to the local movie house, we were always given the best seats.

But things were not all going well. Pietro and Jimmy did not

Pumpkin Pie

Make a pâte brisée: In a food processor mix 1½ cups sifted flour with 3 tablespoons sugar and 9 tablespoons butter, cut into small pieces. Then add 2 eggs and 1 tablespoon oil and process until all the ingredients are well mixed. With the machine still running, add ¼ cup ice water. The dough will form a ball. Remove the dough, dust it with flour, and wrap it in foil. Refrigerate for 30 minutes. In the food processor place 2 cups pumpkin purée with ½ cup heavy cream, 4 eggs, 2 tablespoons brandy, ½ cup sugar, and ¼ teaspoon cinnamon. Process until all the ingredients are puréed. Butter a tart pan or a 9-inch pie pan. On a floured board roll out the dough. Place the dough in the pie pan, pressing the edges with a fork. Bake the pie crust in a preheated 375-degree oven for 10 minutes. Remove the pie from the oven, pour in the pumpkin purée, and bake it for 40 minutes, or until a knife inserted in the middle comes out clean. Serve the pie at room temperature with whipped cream. Serves 6 to 10.

really get along. The question of salary came up often, and the answers were always vague. Jimmy had not been paid, and his involvement was doubtful. Jimmy was getting more and more upset. One day, after an intense fight with Pietro, Jimmy came home and said, "Let's pack our bags and leave. It's time we went back to the United States. I want to build there. It's my country, not Italy!" And so I said goodbye to all my friends, packed our bags, and sent them on to Paris. We drove off in our little sports car toward Paris. After an hour of driving, I suddenly realized that I had left my turtle under the *stuffa*. "We have to go back," I cried. "I must have her!" We returned to Udine, but the turtle had disappeared. Had she known we were leaving? I was very upset but Signora Baldini comforted me. "It's all right . . . buy another one when you know where you will live. If I find her I will take care of her." I was heart-broken, but Jimmy seemed relieved that there was no turtle to take home. Our troubles were not over, though. Our car suddenly broke down, and it was Jimmy's turn to be broken-hearted, having to sell his Morgan to a local garage. We took the train to Paris.

In Paris, my mother and stepfather helped us find the cheapest way to go to New York—by boat. We booked passage on the *Liberté*, while our belongings were packed up to be shipped on a commercial liner. Clément sadly announced that the revolutionary government had nationalized everything, including the factories in which my father had invested. I had lost my suit and all I received was twenty thousand dollars to take with me to New York. We said our goodbyes and, poorer than I expected, sailed from Le Havre to a new life in New York.

* * *

As the boat left the harbor, I knew I was in trouble. I felt sick, and remembering my last sea voyage (long ago, from Egypt to France), I announced that I could not join Jimmy in the cabin below, and that I would have to stay on deck. Unable to eat anything, wrapped in blankets, I spent the six-day crossing feeling miserable despite the fact that Jimmy spent most of the day taking care of me. He prepared me for our arrival by talking about his family. He spoke about his mother, Anne, whom I had met at our wedding, and who was now living eight months of the year in Coral Gables, Florida, spending the summers in New York. Murray, Jimmy's brother, whom I also knew, was now a member of the *New York Times* editorial board and lived with his wife, Naima, and two very young sons, Maxwell and John, in a large apartment on the Upper West Side. We were going to stay with them for a few days until Jimmy found a job and an apartment. He also talked of his aunts, Edie and Gina, two spinsters whom he doted on. The night before we arrived in New York, the captain announced that the city had experienced an unexpected snowstorm and that seven inches of snow had fallen. Jimmy told me that we had to catch a glimpse of the Statue of Liberty as the boat approached New York Harbor. At five o'clock, on a cloudy, gray day on the first of April, the statue stood waving her snow-topped torch. I gripped Jimmy's hand tightly, wondering what our life would be like in this new country.

Anne and Murray greeted us as we disembarked, but they looked rather grim. As we drove through the city, we learned that Jimmy's favorite aunt, Edie, had died a few days before. While they talked, I looked around. After Paris, New York looked gray, ugly, and dirty. The snow, piled on the edges of the sidewalks, had already turned brown. My sense of foreboding grew as we approached the west side of Manhattan. We arrived in front of a magnificent building with large columns facing a garden enclosing another very large building that looked like a Parisian palace. "It's the Museum of Natural History," Murray volunteered. Its grandeur reassured me, and I began to feel better as we rode an old-fashioned elevator to the sixth floor of Murray's apartment, across the street from the museum. At the door a charming little boy welcomed me. Maxwell was seven, and I liked him right away but I fell completely in love with his fifteen-month-old brother, John. I was twenty-two and wanted a child—and here was a baby who looked like my husband and took to me very quickly. We settled down and over the next several days, Jimmy showed me New York. The weather changed, and New York's famous blue sky and the sun shining on its skyscrapers began to work their magic. Life promised to be interesting and fun if I could get out of my in-laws' apartment. To begin with, the food was a problem. I got used to white toast for breakfast, but American coffee was horribly weak compared to the rich Italian brew I was accustomed to. Naima, my new British sister-in-law, made strong English tea for me instead. When my mother-in-law prepared lunch, it was invariably a tuna fish sandwich on white bread. The tuna fish, to my horror and disgust, was mixed with some sort of sweet mayonnaise and celery. The bread became soggy, and I had to pretend a violent stomachache in order not to eat it. Dinner was served around seven, much too early for me, even if I had had no lunch. If Naima cooked, I asked if I could help, and together we managed to make some very good meals: coq au vin, *blanquette de veau, real* French fries. Later I won Maxwell's heart by making golden crêpes stuffed with jam at least twice a week. But if it was my mother-in-law's turn to cook, I had to face soft vegetables and stewed meats swimming in greasy sauces. She made an orange gelatin (Jell-O, I later discovered) with bits of carrot floating inside it, or a baked ham with pineapple and brown sugar. I couldn't get used to the excessive sweetness mingling with the savory, and I usually stuck with her oft-served baked potatoes, which she left alone. Anne's walnut cookies, however, were fabulous—rich yet delicate—but she never divulged the recipe and only made them when she knew I was out. After a month of living with them, I had lost about fifteen pounds and liked myself! I was slender for the first time in my life.

Only two weeks after our arrival, Jimmy found a job, left early every morning, and often worked Saturdays. One such Saturday, he asked me to join him at lunch so he could introduce me to his co-workers. Everyone called me "Colette," which I found strange—no one in France would have called me by my given name the first time they met me. It took me a couple of years to get used to this friendly way of greeting someone I just met. We went to a local luncheonette, and Jimmy told me that the best thing there was a hamburger. In Paris we had *steak haché* from time to time, and I did like the sautéed ground steak, so I said I would try a hamburger cooked rare. I took a bite of mine and it was well done. So I snapped my fingers and said, "Garçon, please, this is not good. I asked for a rare hamburger." Jimmy blushed, terribly embarrassed in front of the others, and whispered, "Don't say that," but I insisted. And under the stares of Jimmy's colleagues, the waiter took away my hamburger and five minutes later, brought me a new hamburger, freshly cooked to perfection. "Delicious," I said with a smile, and everyone laughed at my pleasure. The next day Jimmy told me that everyone had been sick. The hamburgers were from the day before and had spoiled. I was the only one who had been served a freshly cooked one.

During the week, I offered to take John to the playground. Naima explained that I could place him in the sandbox or on a swing. Mothers minding their children approached me and plied me with questions about Naima and her husband. I tried to be polite, but after a few times, I told Naima that I didn't want to go to the playground anymore. I was not used to so much familiarity (and nosiness) and I did not like it. Instead, I took John for walks in the neighborhood. Supermarkets baffled me. I stared at cuts of meat wrapped in plastic and wondered what they were, realizing that there wasn't a butcher to tell me what was good that day. Vegetables and salads were even more difficult to choose from. The string beans looked overgrown and the tomatoes were pale and smelled like plastic. I couldn't find shallots or tarragon or chervil; the only fresh herb was parsley. How was I going to cook? Worst of all was the bread. It was just a *pain de mie* (crustless white bread), sliced by machine and stuffed into plastic bags. At least I found out that Jewish stores sold good, crusty rye bread. And I liked the rich American milk, which I downed by the glass. I always say that I grew an inch taller when I arrived. I liked bacon, not for breakfast but on bread with sliced cucumbers. I discovered bagels and bialys, smoked salmon and smoked whitefish. Every day on our walk I bought a salt bagel for me and an egg bagel for John and we ate them in the street. When Jimmy came home at night, I tried to pretend that I was content, but I was truly bored. I had to leave my in-laws' apartment, get one for us, get a job, or go to school. I asked Naima to help me find an apartment quickly and she discovered a small one two blocks away, with a small living room, a dinette—what Jimmy called a closet to eat in—a kitchenette (I was beginning to feel extra small with the name Colette), and a small bedroom (or sleepette?). Jimmy hated it because the windows overlooked a wall, but I just wanted to be in my own house, alone with my husband, my books, my food, and my own real life. And so we moved in with a bed, a small table, two chairs, and five huge straw baskets from France containing my trousseau. As I unpacked, I caressed the lovely linen sheets that Tante Beca had so carefully chosen for me. Could I really use them here? I had no maid to wash them, just a washing machine down the hall, which would ruin them. I put them away. There were dozens of tablecloths. Did she really think I was going to entertain that much? Suddenly, I longed to see my

Egyptian family, to hear Ahmet's voice calling me into the kitchen to taste something he had just made. I cried, then repacked the linens, closed the baskets, and set them aside. I decided that New York was my new home and I was going to live the way my new family did.

A few days after we moved in, I looked in the *New York Times* for a job and found an ad that required someone who spoke and wrote French but could also read and understand English. I immediately called the office and talked to a man who gave me an appointment for the next day. I took the subway alone to the interview, and I got the job right away. I would be paid fifty dollars a week to read all the newspapers published in New York, between 9 A.M. and 2 P.M. On Fridays I was to send by telex to the French newspaper a summary of the most interesting things I had read in the papers. On my first day, Mr. Roland handed me the *New York Times*, the *Herald Tribune*, the *Post*, the *Wall Street Journal*, and the *Daily News* and told me to start reading. I discovered how exciting and unusual America was. There were problems with the city, a mayoral election was coming up, Eisenhower was president, Congress was fraught with infighting, and there were multiple political scandals erupting. The most interesting of the papers was the *Wall Street Journal*. Every day its front page carried a small article about something extraordinary or bizarre or fun happening somewhere in the United States. I read the women's page in the *New York Times*, learned about avant-garde theater, fashion, musicals. On Friday, I wrote a synopsis of the week and sent it to Paris. I was finally becoming familiar with New York. In the afternoon I took a bus all the way downtown to the Lower East Side and walked down Essex Street. There I could buy fresh butter, excellent bread, pickles, good olives, and dried fruit just like in Egypt. I discovered Bleecker Street and the Italian merchants, who sold fresh lettuce, delicious salami, prosciutto, and fresh pasta. I realized I did not have to buy meat in the supermarket, but found a good butcher who tried to cut meat as I liked it. I started to cook as I did in Munich and in Udine for Jimmy's new friends.

As Christmas got nearer, Anne wrote from Florida that we should come and spend the holiday with her. She wanted to introduce us, the young couple, to her friends. We agreed. Coral Gables was then a rather small, provincial town near Miami. Anne's house was set in a large garden filled with lemon, orange, and mango trees. The mango trees reminded me of Cairo, and the Spanish-style house was comfortable and pleasant. The first evening there, I was in for a surprise. Jimmy drove me to his favorite restaurant to try barbecued ribs for the first time. All my prejudices against American cuisine melted away as I sank my teeth into a juicy smoked rib! I had never tasted anything so delicious. I ate ten of them, sauce dripping from my chin, drinking beer, and having a great time. The next day Anne announced that her women friends were inviting me, and only me, to a luncheon in a Miami hotel. I had never been to an all-women's lunch, and the thought amused me. As we entered the private dining room, I found myself surrounded by a dozen women all about my mother-in-law's age, who greeted me with little cries of "How charming . . . What a lovely accent . . . Would you look at her eyes!" One woman handed me an orchid in a plastic box; it was beautiful, and I was afraid it might die before I got home. I looked around, grabbed a glass of water, and placed the orchid in it. Several ladies frowned and clucked; the lady who had given me the orchid looked puzzled, and Anne bent down and whispered to me, "It's a corsage. You're supposed to pin it on your blouse!" Embarrassed, I apologized, pinned the ridiculous, smelly flower on my blouse, and sat down to lunch.

On Christmas Eve, Anne's best friend gave a large dinner dance in our honor. We arrived late to the party, which had been going on for at least an hour. We were introduced as an exotic couple, a French-Egyptian wife married to Anne's successful son. Guests had drunk a lot, and soon I found myself surrounded by a group of men saying things like, "You know, Frenchmen take two hours for lunch . . . can you imagine!" And "The French are not as hardworking as we are," and "Those French forgot that we won the war for them." This went on for an hour, until I couldn't bear the humiliation and insisted that Jimmy take me home. Christmas had always been for me something I longed for—a family affair with a Christmas tree and lots of presents all around it. In my fantasy, children sang carols and I'd make a wonderful dinner that we would eat at midnight. The house was cold when we returned, and I was shivering with anger and hurt, so Jimmy built a fire and took me in his arms, kissing me lovingly. "You will have your dream soon," he whispered. "Let's make love on the carpet here, near the fire; let's make a baby." We made love with passionate abandon that night, and I fell asleep knowing that I was going to have a child. Whatever life had in store for us, I was ready.

Back in New York, I soon found out that I was pregnant. I immediately wrote my mother. To my surprise, she wrote back that she was thrilled. Her letters came weekly, with inquiries about my health, my needs, and the baby's name. A month before the birth, she asked me if she could come, and I was secretly pleased. I was lonely and needed a friend. My mother arrived with several suitcases, and I was afraid that she would stay with us for months but did not dare ask her. As we brought her back to our tiny two-bedroom apartment, I was worried that she would criticize it, but she seemed quite happy to be in New York with us. I left her alone to unpack, and when I returned half an hour later, the bed was covered with piles of baby gifts—knitted frocks, daintily embroidered linen sheets, hand-crocheted bonnets, starched bibs, and booties in all the colors of a pastel rainbow. "Where did you find all these lovely things?" I asked, picking up a linen sheet embroidered with tiny little rabbits and turtles. "Grace of Monaco is expecting a baby, just like you, and she's due about the same time. Did you know that *Paris Match* published the baby's trousseau?" No, I did not. My mother had decided that her grandchild should have all the things that Grace of Monaco had ordered for her child. I kissed my mother fondly. I was very happy.

Two weeks after my mother's arrival, Marianne was born. Five days later I was back home, tired but happy and proud of my tiny baby. As I entered the apartment, I saw a magnificent, enormous baby carriage standing in the middle of the living room. "It is an English pram," my mother explained. "Clément and I thought that Marianne should have the best . . . the Rolls-Royce of carriages!" My smile covered up my dismay; I was thinking how difficult it would be for me to take it in and out of the elevator! One night, exhausted from the endless round of breast-feeding, I woke up to Marianne's desperate crying—the hoarse sobs that come after many minutes of wailing. I rose in a panic, only to find my mother rocking the baby and singing her a song, effectively soothing her. It wasn't time to feed her, so I tiptoed back to bed thinking that if I did not have the type of mother I had wanted, at least Marianne would have a great grandmother. And it turned out to be true.

When Marianne was eight months old, my stepfather insisted that the three of us come to Maison Laffitte, a then rural suburb outside Paris, where he and my mother had a large house. Jimmy had been working very hard and needed a break, so we decided to accept his offer. This time Jimmy insisted that I have a new wardrobe and for the first time ever, he took me shopping. He chose elegant dresses, shoes, and a decadent hat. "I want you to look beautiful," he told me earnestly. "I want your family to admire my lovely wife and how America transformed her into an elegant young woman. I want to show them that we are not a country of barbarians!" I laughed at his pleasure. I was delighted, happy, and proud to show off my husband and my new baby to my friends and my family.

When we arrived in Paris, Mira fell in love with my baby girl and played with her in their garden. My mother decided that Jimmy and I needed a vacation and announced that she would take care of Marianne. We were free to explore Paris together. That night, Jimmy and I walked down the Champs Elysées to Le Jour et La Nuit, the restaurant where we had eaten dinner four years ago. It was there that we had decided to spend our lives together. I don't remember what we ate but it must have been magic, for our marriage has so far lasted forty-seven years.

Acknowledgments

I want to thank my husband and my children for all the support they gave me while I wrote this book. I have special thanks for my daughter Marianne who read the manuscript and gave me much needed criticism, and who nudged me along when the events of September 11 made everything seem futile. I want to express my gratitude and thanks to my wonderful editor, Rosemary Ahern, and to my English editor, Alexandra Pringle, who trusted me to write a sequel to *Apricots on the Nile*. My deep appreciation to my agent and friend, Gloria Loomis, who worked so hard to make things happen for me.

Return to Paris

A Memoir

Colette Rossant

A Readers Club Guide

ABOUT THIS GUIDE

The suggested questions are intended to help your reading group find new and interesting angles and topics for discussion for Colette Rossant's *Return to Paris*. We hope that these ideas will enrich your conversation and increase your enjoyment of the book.

Many fine books from Washington Square Press feature Readers Club Guides. For a complete listing, or to read the Guides online, visit http://www.BookClubReader.com.

Questions and Topics for Discussion

1. *Return to Paris* is at once an evocative food memoir, an adolescent girl's poignant coming-of-age story, and travel writing set in the gastronomic capital of the world in the aftermath of World War II. Discuss the ways in which the book succeeds or fails on each of these levels.

2. Colette Rossant, who has won a James Beard Award for her food writing, has been hailed as the literary heir to M. F. K. Fisher. Do you agree or disagree? Why? Who are the food writers Rossant most reminds you of?

3. Thinking back to her life in Cairo, and her despair after her father died and her mother deserted her, Colette writes: *"I was devastated and heartbroken. Ahmet and his kitchen became my only solace as he enveloped me with love and food."* Later, when her mother moves her back to Paris, the kitchen once again is the room to which she retreats. Discuss the emotional role that the kitchen has played in Colette's life. Why do you think many people regard the kitchen as a sanctuary? What memories of your own are tied to the kitchen?

4. Even though her mother repeatedly lies to, betrays, and abandons her, and she describes life in her grandmother's enormous apartment as *"often grim, loveless, and cold,"* Colette never seems dispirited or depressed. How does the author manage to keep the tone of her memoir upbeat?

5. Throughout the memoir Colette recalls the comfort that she has found in various foods. As you were reading the book, were you surprised that the first recipe she included was for Cucumber Salad, a dish that is not one most Americans traditionally think of as a "comfort food"? Do you believe that certain foods actually bring comfort more than others? How much of the comfort they provide is because of the memories we attach to them?

6. Colette's life definitely takes a turn upward when her mother marries. At the restaurant where she meets her new stepfather, Colette is introduced to her first truffle, *"an epiphany of the senses, a thrill caressing my adolescent tongue. . . ."* Next she discovers quenelles: *"As I took a bite, I had a second revelation. The airy quenelle dissolved into nothing, leaving my mouth with a creamy, buttery sensation hinting of the sea. . . ."* Talk about Colette Rossant's ability to convey the intoxicating pleasure she derives from food.

7. What does Mira mean when he tells Colette "food is memory"? If you were to close your eyes and try to iden-

tify all the ingredients of a new dish that you taste for the first time, as Mira encourages Colette to do, how successful do you think you would be? Do you think it matters? One cannot cook a dish without knowing the ingredients, but is such recognition necessary in order to savor food? Do you think the ability to appreciate exquisite taste sensations is a special gift or a learned response? Discuss whether or not certain dishes actually are superior to others—or if it is simply a matter of which you prefer.

8. One of the most amusing scenes in the memoir is when Georges and Gérard declare that they are both in love with sixteen-year-old Colette and suggest that she choose between them by kissing them each in turn. How does the kissing contest remind you of a food tasting? What do you think of this method of selecting a boyfriend?

9. When Colette scandalizes her French family by announcing her intention to marry an American, only her stepfather, Mira, accepts Jimmy without reservation. But when Colette becomes pregnant, her mother is transformed. The cold, withholding woman who never had time for her daughter, who repeatedly abandoned her, suddenly can't wait to become a doting grandmother. Why do you think her mother is ready to be loving and nurturing toward her grandchild? Why do you think Colette is able

to accept this without resentment? Do you think you could?

10. "How foody does a memoir about eating have to be?" one reviewer asks, and answers her own question by stating: *"If it were up to me, each paragraph would minutely describe ambrosial meals, perhaps alternated with passages about picking tomatoes in the sun."* If it were up to you, where would you draw the line? Is it possible for an author to obsess about food too much? At what point does eating to escape one's loneliness and unhappiness border on an eating disorder? *"Colette Rossant can make a ham sandwich sound like a delicacy, and describe a raspberry tart with the same passion that others talk about their love affairs,"* another reviewer comments. Do you think it is appropriate to talk about food with the same passion that people talk about their love affairs? Why or why not?

11. How do you enjoy the "food memoir" as a genre? What do you think of the recipes the author weaves into her memoir? Have you tried them? Are you tempted to? Are they smoothly incorporated into the narrative? If you had to choose two or three favorite recipes from this book, which would they be? Why?

12. *"Her memories are vividly rendered, infused with piquant tastes and smells, like that of roasting pigeons mixed with*

cumin and limes. *Nostalgia for the Egypt of Rossant's childhood pervades this charming book,*" wrote the *New York Times* of the author's previous food memoir, *Apricots on the Nile.* If you have read both books, how would you compare them? If you did not read the earlier memoir, are you now likely to? Why or why not?